Insure
Sensibly

A Guide to Life and
Disability Insurance

JAMES BULLOCK & GEORGE BRETT

THE GLOBE AND MAIL

Penguin Books

PENGUIN BOOKS
Published by the Penguin Group
Penguin Books Canada Ltd., 10 Alcorn Avenue, Suite 300, Toronto, Canada M4V 3B2
Penguin Books Ltd., 27 Wrights Lane, London W8 5TZ, England
Viking Penguin Inc., 40 West 23rd Street, New York, New York 10010, U.S.
Penguin Books Australia Ltd., Ringwood, Victoria, Australia
Penguin Books (NZ) Ltd., 182-190 Wairau Road, Auckland 10, New Zealand
Penguin Books Ltd., Registered Offices: Harmondsworth, Middlesex, England

Published in Penguin Books, 1995

10 9 8 7 6 5 4 3 2 1

Canadian Cataloguing in Publication Data
The National Library of Canada has catalogued this publication as follows:
Bullock, James, 1944-
    Insure sensibly
(Financial times personal finance library)
Annual.
Description based on: 1992.
Issues for 1995- ... published in the series: Globe and Mail personal finance library.
Following title: A guide to life and disability insurance.
ISSN 1193-8943
ISBN 0-14-025543-5 (1995)

1. Insurance, Life – Periodicals. 2. Insurance, Disability – Periodicals.
I. Brett, George, 1938-1992 II. Title. III.Title: Financial times. IV. Series.
V. Series: Globe and Mail personal finance library

HG8773.B84   368.3'2'005   C93-030701-1

Cover design: Creative Network
Cover illustration: Peter Yundt

CONTENTS

Tables and Illustrations

Introduction

IF A FORTY-YEAR-OLD MAN IS sold $500,000 of life insurance, he could face a monthly premium of $36 a month if he buys a policy from Reliable Life Insurance Co. If he buys it from The Empire Life Insurance Co., he might pay $797.85 a month. How can this be? Is Empire's policy tremendously overpriced? Is Reliable Life a fly-by-night company trying to snare customers with cheap insurance? Not at all. Empire Life's policy is well priced for that type of insurance – whole life. The policy sold by Reliable Life, a reputable firm with a long history of serving Canadians, is one-year term insurance – and a good price for its kind. In the end, they offer the same immediate protection – $500,000 payable upon death – yet they're radically different.

Which policy, then, should you buy?

The life insurance industry uses a string of "ifs," "ands" or "buts" to explain the tremendous differences in the cost of life insurance – and the bewildering array of different policies. In the end, few people understand the cost of life insurance, thereby making it difficult for them to know which is the best value.

Then there is the question of how much life insurance to buy. In 1994, new policy purchases of life insurance by Canadian households averaged $100,600. The average total life insurance (including group and individual policies) owned by Canadian households was $177,300. If you died and left this insurance to your husband or wife – along with a mortgage to pay and children to raise – would he or she be able to cope? It's obviously far too little insurance for most people, but how much is enough? And what kind should you buy?

Canada has 148 life insurance companies selling thousands of variations of life insurance policies. To buy these policies, Canadians paid $9.1 billion in life insurance premiums in 1994, an average of $96,300 per insured person. Did they get their money's worth? Some did. Many did not. Some bought enough insurance but paid too much for it – wasting money they could probably have spent with greater satisfaction on other things. Others bought far too little insurance – and their families could suffer financial hardship if they died.

People make mistakes in buying insurance because they lack the knowledge to determine their own needs or to choose a policy from among the many choices. It's not easy. The choices in the life insurance market can confuse even highly educated professionals because policies that seem to be the same can be so different. But understanding life insurance is not as difficult as you might think. Using ordinary language and simple arithmetic, *Insure Sensibly* will tell you how to determine your life and disability insurance needs – and buy the policy that most effectively serves those needs.

Part One examines life insurance needs, taking you step by step through your financial life to determine how much insurance you should buy. Part Two demystifies the life insurance market by looking at the basic kinds of life insurance – term, whole life, term-to-100, and universal life. To do this, we take you through the details of a life insurance policy, explaining in plain English the meaning and significance of each clause.

Part Three takes you shopping. It looks at the ways insurance is sold, the price of policies, the application form, and the people who sell insurance – the agents and brokers. Finally, we look at the sensitive issue of replacing an existing policy.

Part Four turns to disability insurance. Insurance industry statistics show that close to a third of all thirty-five-year-olds will be disabled for at least six months before reaching age sixty-five. Almost half of those people will still be disabled, at least slightly, after five years. Although 7.7 million Canadians are protected by long-term disability insurance, much of that protection is so inadequate it could leave many exposed to financial hardship.

Insure Sensibly takes a close look at the financial protection available to most working Canadians – unemployment insurance, workers' compensation, the Canada or Quebec Pension Plan, and auto insurance – and at the group plan offered by your employer. Unfortunately, for too many Canadians, especially executives and professionals, the income from these plans would not be enough. To protect yourself and your family, you may need individual disability insurance, an intimidating and complex product. *Insure Sensibly* will unravel its mysteries, making it possible for you to ensure that you, and your family, are well protected.

Part Five looks at the life and disability insurance marketplace. You'll gain an insight into how insurance companies make their money – and how to protect your own.

Acknowledgments

The authors would like to thank the following for their help in preparing this book:

Robert Barney, president, Compulife Software Inc., Kitchener, Ontario.

Kenneth Beattie of Ideal Insurance Brokers Inc., Willowdale, Ontario.

Minnie Lawrence, a partner in the chartered accounting firm of Orenstein & Partners, Toronto.

Helen Nerska, director of marketing, Paul Revere Life Insurance Co., Burlington, Ontario.

We would also like to commend our editor, Elaine Wyatt, for her dedication and enthusiasm.

This book was written as a joint effort by myself, who supplied the technical knowledge, and George Brett, a man skilled at converting techno-babble to readable, interesting and useful prose.

At the time, both George and I were suffering from depression. This is a mental disorder that does not necessarily present symptoms of being melancholy. In our cases, neither of us was feeling very sad, but we both had our share of problems. I don't recall telling George much of anything of my problems, and he only gave me a glimpse of his.

We were both faced with financial problems as a direct result of our mental problems. I was collecting $9,000 a month in tax-free disability from my personal disability policies. This went a long way to solving the problems caused by a dramatic reduction in earned income. George had life insurance, but no disability insurance that would pay him while he was depressed. He elected to quiet his demons, and trigger his life insurance death benefits.

I am now well on the road to recovery, and able to aid – for the first time – in the annual revision of *Insure Sensibly*. As I read George's words, I can't help but think that not only have his words withstood the tests of time and hindsight, but I find myself thinking that my recovery, and, indeed, my life may be due to the adequacy of my insurance. These are not subjects taught to agents, nor are they thoughts I can adequately explain here or to my clients.

Jim Bullock
September 1995

CHAPTER 1

Who Really Needs Life Insurance?

WHAT DO YOU FEEL IS YOUR most important asset? Your home? Your registered retirement savings plan? Your portfolio of investments? For most people, it's none of these things. Your most important asset is almost certainly your ability to earn an income. Many people put a good deal of thought into insuring their houses, cars, fur coats and power boats while giving scant attention to the asset that pays for these things: their earnings.

And so we come to the misnamed financial product called life insurance. It is not your life you are insuring but the economic value of your life, specifically your future income. Can you afford to lose your future income? Of course you can. If you die, you won't need money. Would others need your income? This is the key issue, because life insurance is the most unselfish type of insurance purchased. A young person's future income is valuable, but death would remove any need for the income. Marriage, and certainly parenthood, changes the need pattern. So, too, does debt. Many people take out life insurance to ensure that their debts, particularly a mortgage, will be paid if they die. Finally, life insurance is used in business to avoid the legal and financial difficulties with bankers and families that could arise if one of the partners dies.

If your death would cause economic hardship to others, you probably need life insurance. At its core, life insurance is very simple. A life insurance policy is bought because the death of a particular person might cause an economic loss during the existence of the policy. The person who buys the policy is the "owner" or "policyholder"; the person whose life is insured is the "insured." They are often, but not always, the same person. If the person does die, the insurance company will have to pay a stipulated sum of money. This sum of money is called the "face value" or "death benefit." It is paid to the people, company or charity named in the policy as the "beneficiary."

Insurance and families

Marriage, among other things, is an economic partnership. Either there is one income or, more often these days, two. It is in the traditional one-income family that the non-working spouse is more vulnerable. One partner, usually the woman, sacrifices her career to devote herself to raising children while her husband works to bring home the family's income. If the husband dies, she is left with the mortgage, debts, and the normal household expenses and obligations, along with all of the responsibilities of parenting – but no income, and perhaps the need to upgrade her skills before she can start earning one.

It is exactly this problem that an adequate amount of life insurance solves. Sufficient life insurance on the working husband ensures the family's future financial security. For less than $400 a year, the couple could buy a life insurance policy that would guarantee the young mother $400,000 in cash, tax-free, at her husband's death to pay off all the bills and provide her with an investment income.

She could then pursue a career compatible with the time demands of being a single mother, and the combination of the income she earns and the investment income would allow her to raise her family in a reasonable lifestyle. She could replace the car once in a while, and take the children on vacation.

In families where these roles are reversed, the insurance would obviously be required on the female breadwinner.

The need for life insurance is often less recognized in two-income families. This is a mistake. For the large majority of such families, both incomes are necessary, so both incomes must be insured. As with one-income families, the insurance should be in proportion to the income at risk.

In most families, life insurance needs are high for the first fifteen or twenty years of marriage, and then might gradually decline as the family's wealth becomes more significant. We say "might" decline because for many families, the needs never decline. They can even increase as one set of obligations replaces another. In particular, it is common for the equity in one house to be rolled into a larger home with a larger, and more threatening, mortgage.

Even the well-being of an older, more established family might be financially threatened if the death of husband or wife triggered a large capital gains tax. In Canada, our capital assets, with the exception of principal residences, are subject to a capital gains tax. (The $100,000 lifetime exemption has been eliminated but there is still a $500,000 lifetime exemption for owners of family businesses.)

Insurance in retirement planning

Life insurance can play a significant role in a couple's retirement planning, especially if most of the retirement income will come from a pension or an annuity purchased with RRSP funds. When you retire, you'll have to choose between a pension income that will last for as long as either you and your husband or wife are alive or an income that will last only until you die, then stop. Unfortunately, the joint income is about 30 percent less than the income on one person's life.

However, if you have permanent life insurance on the life of the pension or RRSP owner, you can choose the higher single-life income, secure in the knowledge that the life insurance death benefit will become available at death. This is a strategy that must be built into your financial plans when you're less than fifty-five years old; even at that age the husband or wife without a pension must be at least five or ten years younger than the pensioner. It doesn't work at all if you try to put it in place while you're in the throes of retiring and scrambling to make up for an inadequate pension or retirement pool of savings.

Let's look at a couple: he's fifty-five years old, she's only forty-five. By the time he's sixty-five, they'll have $500,000 in RRSPs, with which they intend to buy a life annuity. Using the annuity rates available in the summer of 1994, they could expect to receive $3,636 a month from a joint-life annuity or $4,861 a month from an annuity on his life alone.

If they buy a $500,000 permanent life insurance policy while he's still fifty-five years old, the premiums will be $655 a month if he doesn't smoke, $1,027 if he does. At retirement, they can choose a single-life annuity and their monthly income, after paying premiums, will be $4,206 – $570 more a month than if he buys a joint-life annuity. When he dies and the annuity income stops, his widow would receive the $500,000 death benefit and could buy an annuity on her own life. If he dies ten years after retiring, she will only be sixty-five. The annuity purchased would give her an income of

$4,343 a month for the rest of her life. If he died at age eighty, when she's seventy, her annuity would provide an income of $4,863 a month. Thus, they will both enjoy a higher income while he's alive and she will continue to have a better income after he's died.

If they wait until he's sixty-five before buying the life insurance policy, his premiums will jump to $1,235 a month. Their income from the single-life annuity after paying premiums will drop to $3,626, $10 less than they would receive from a joint-life annuity. Clearly, planning ahead is important.

Insurance in business

The death of the family breadwinner means a vital future income is lost. The death of a homemaker usually requires the hiring of a housekeeper or nanny, and perhaps reduced career opportunities as the survivor devotes more attention to parental responsibilities.

The death of a business owner triggers problems with the bank, which is worried about the company's line of credit, and with surviving business partners, who have lost the deceased's contributions of time, talent and money. They are often left negotiating with the surviving spouse who still wants income, but has little or nothing to contribute.

If the owner dies, and leaves the business to the family, an interesting meeting takes place. The family approaches the bank to arrange to continue the relationship, while the banker decides to reduce the line of credit and see how the family manages the business. This situation can create a financial crisis that ruins the business, especially if there is substantial cash needed to pay capital gains tax.

For this reason, most business owners are insured through a policy owned by the company, quite apart from the insurance they buy for their families' benefit. This arrangement guarantees the bank that the business loans would be paid off, or at least substantially reduced, if the owner dies. It also gives the new owners – his family – a chance to run the business with a reduced debt load.

If the business owner has partners, they probably life insure each other, so that at death the surviving partners have the cash to buy the deceased's shares from the estate or family. A shareholders' agreement usually spells out the details of the buy-out. In the absence of such an agreement, the surviving partners might suddenly find that they have the deceased's surviving spouse as a new partner. This person may know nothing about the business, but might need a full income.

On the other hand, the surviving spouse might want to sell out, but the partners might not be able to raise the money. After the death of a partner, the bank may have misgivings. Even if the loan is extended, the cost will be high because the remaining partners must repay the loan with after-tax earnings. Paying off the loan, with interest, might cost two or three times the amount borrowed.

The solution is an insurance policy on the partner's life for the full cost of the agreed-upon purchase price. This would immediately guarantee the partner's estate that the funds would be available to pay for the purchase. The cost of insurance would be only from 0.5 percent to 2 percent a year of the purchase price, depending on the partner's age and the type of policy purchased. This answer to the problem is both guaranteed and affordable, and the capital never has to be paid back.

There is another use for life insurance in business. Some businesses prosper because of the unique talents of a key individual. If the business would suffer financial losses in the event of this person's death, the answer is "key person" insurance that would provide the business with a financial cushion at this person's death. (The business uses of life insurance are explored further in chapter thirteen.)

People buy life insurance as security for their families, as part of retirement planning, and as a key component of business financing. In the next chapter, we will discuss one of the most vital questions you must answer about life insurance: How much life insurance do you need?

CHAPTER 2

How Much Insurance Do You Need?

SINCE LIFE INSURANCE IS bought – in families, at least – to protect the people you love, it is crucial that you buy enough insurance to meet their needs. You will want the death benefit to be large enough to ensure your family can continue to live in their own world without struggling to satisfy their day-to-day needs. You'll want them to be able to pay the unexpected costs that will arise from your death; and you'll want them to be able to rebuild their life without the burden of debt. The amount your family will need is not only uniquely individual but will change as time passes.

The finances of most families evolve from a time when there are few investments and heavy debts to a retirement funded by investments and a pension. Financial independence should be your long-term financial plan, but should death intervene before this is achieved, your survivors could be left in serious economic trouble. Because of this harsh reality, you have to work for the best while preparing for the worst – you have to have life insurance.

The worksheet in this chapter will help you determine exactly how much insurance you need. That amount depends on your family's needs, the earning ability of your husband or wife, your investments, and your debts. If your husband or wife is wealthy, concern about your future income may not be important. In all other situations, it is important and should be insured. Don't take your insurance agent's word for it; and don't accept an arbitrary formula like five or ten times your salary. Your family's security rests on there being enough cash at death. On the other hand, the advice, "If in doubt, guess high. No one ever complained about having too much life insurance," diminishes your ability to build your wealth. After all, every dollar spent on insurance is a dollar lost to your investment program. Buy just the right amount of coverage. You can only be sure of doing this by taking the time – and it will take time – to calculate your insurance needs accurately.

There will be some help for your family from the government. If you have contributed to the Canada or Quebec Pension Plan, your surviving spouse and children will be eligible for a government pension. The monthly benefit usually depends on your contributions and the age of the survivors. In mid-1994, a surviving spouse age sixty-five or older received a maximum benefit of $417 a month from the CPP or QPP. Under the CPP, the maximum benefit to a survivor under age sixty-five was $385. Under the QPP, a surviving spouse received up to $660 if aged fifty-five to sixty-four; $579 if under age fifty-five. Surviving children up to age eighteen, or up to age twenty-five if attending school full-time, were entitled to a maximum monthly benefit of $160.47 from the CPP or $50.95 from the QPP. Children who lose both working parents can claim the CPP or QPP benefit twice.

As you go through the worksheet, keep in mind that your insurance is intended to relieve your family of any financial worries, both at their time of bereavement and as their lives settle back into their then usual lifestyle. If there are two income earners in your family, the worksheet should be completed twice to determine the insurance needs of each person. Your family will need money for four reasons:

- to pay the expenses that will arise from your death – your funeral, the legal fees and unpaid taxes
- to create an income that will help cover their day-to-day living expenses
- to pay off your debts. Being debt-free, your family will not only be financially secure, they will have fewer day-to-day expenses to worry about.
- to create a financial cushion to protect them against unexpected expenses and to pay special expenses, such as your children's university tuition.

Your step-by-step insurance calculations
Step one: Your family's assets
The question, "How much life insurance do I need?" can't be answered until you answer another pressing question, "What resources would my family have, after all my debts were paid, if I died tomorrow?" That answer encompasses any insurance you have

already, survivor benefits your family would receive from your pension, and any assets you own that could be sold and invested to generate income.

It's important to keep that distinction in mind. You probably own plenty of things that are valuable but don't produce an income. Your house, car, boat and cottage seldom provide any income to your family. In fact, your home and cottage actually consume income through maintenance, heat, light and insurance. Unless your family would sell the car, boat or cottage, these should be left out of your insurance-planning calculations.

Be conservative in estimating the value of any stocks, bonds or mutual funds. The market could be down at the time your family is forced to sell them if, indeed, you or they want them sold. Don't include your RRSP investments; these will be needed by your husband or wife at retirement.

Step two: Your final expenses and special needs
Your family will need money to pay for your funeral – probably at least $5,000. (Funerals rise in price just like everything else; this is a figure you should review every time you review your insurance needs.) Your family will have to settle your estate. There will be the legal costs of probate. This is the official process that ensures the validity of your will, watches over the payment of your debts and taxes, and ensures that the instructions in your will are fulfilled.

Your family will also have to settle your affairs with Revenue Canada, quite apart from the tax owed in the year you die. At death, Revenue Canada considers all of your assets to have been sold, triggering the capital gains tax on their increase in value. (However, there is a tax deferral on your wealth and possessions that pass to your husband or wife.) To ensure your estate pays as little tax as possible on your final income tax return, make sure your family will have enough money to seek an accountant's advice. You should count on legal and accounting bills of at least $10,000.

Your life insurance and personal debts insurance benefits should pay any outstanding balances on your debts. This includes your mortgage, credit card balances, loans from friends, and car loans. Parents who would like their children to be able to attend university or college should ensure the dream doesn't die with their own demise. Tuition and living expenses have been soaring. The Canadian Scholarship Trust Foundation, which sells registered education savings plans, estimates it takes at least $7,000 a year to send

Life Insurance Planning Worksheet

Step one: Your family's assets	Value in $
1. Death benefit of life insurance already owned	
2. Death benefit of pension	
3. Investments	
Mutual funds	
Stocks	
Bonds	
Canada Savings Bonds	
GICs or term deposits	
Real estate	
4. Assets that could be sold and invested	
5. Your bank balances	
A. Total assets at death	

Step two: Your final expenses and special needs	
1. The funeral	
2. Legal and accounting fees	
3. Income and capital gains tax	
4. Your debts	
Mortgage	
Credit cards	
Car loan	
Other	
5. Education fund	
6. Comfort fund & special needs	
7. Emergency fund	
B. Total final expenses and special needs	

a student to university – tuition, room and board, books, transportation and other expenses. Remember that variables such as location and course of study will affect the cost and that these costs tend to increase from year to year.

Finally, it's impossible for you to anticipate every expense or problem your family might face after your death. The car might need major repairs, the furnace or refrigerator might need to be re-

Step three: Your family's monthly income needs   **Cost in $**

1. Your family's shelter

    Rent/condo fees/house maintenance

    Insurance

    Property taxes

    Utilities and maintenance

2. Food and household supplies

3. Clothing

    Laundry and dry cleaning

4. Utilities

5. Telephone

6. Medical and dental expenses

7. Car insurance and maintenance

8. Child care

9. Entertainment

10. Vacation

11. Other expenses

Total monthly expenses

To determine the monthly income that will have to be generated by the insurance, take the total monthly income your family will require and subtract any income earned by your husband or wife, generated by your investments or provided by the government.

Monthly expenses: $_____

Income earned by your spouse:– $_____

Income from investments:– $_____

Government benefits:– $_____

Extra monthly income needed:= $_____

The next step is to incorporate the number of years your investments will have to last. To do this, multiply the monthly income your family will need to receive from investments by the appropriate factor in the inflation table on the opposite page. Your family's monthly income needs $_____ times the multiplication factor _____ equals _____(C). If your family needs an extra $1,000 a month for fifteen years, they'll have to have $145,000 to invest. If your family needs $1,500 a month for another twenty years, they'll need $270,000 to invest.

Your family's insurance requirements are:

Final expenses and special needs: $_____ B

Investment income required: $_____ C

Total investment pool required   =$_____ (B + C)

Assets and existing insurance   –$_____ A

Insurance required   =$_____

Investment Capital Requirements

Years income must last	Multiply income by
1	7
2	20
3	33
4	45
5	56
6	66
7	76
8	85
9	95
10	104
11	112
12	120
13	128
14	136
15	145
16	152
17	159
18	166
19	173

TABLE I

placed, the roof or basement might start to leak. Give your family an emergency fund of at least $10,000.

Step three: Your family's monthly income needs

Once you are no longer working and bringing home a monthly income, your family will need a pool of capital that it can invest. It is the income from this investment that will replace the income you would have earned had you lived. To determine how large a pool of capital they will need, you must determine how much income they need. When calculating your family's shelter expenses you should include the monthly rent and/or operating costs, but not your mortgage; it will have been paid off by the death benefit. Food and clothing expenses will probably drop, typically by about 25 percent when the family breadwinner dies. Some expenses, like your utilities or home insurance, will remain the same while others, such as child-care expenses, will increase. Others are less certain; they depend on your family and changes in lifestyle that might arise as the family adjusts. For example, will entertainment expenses rise or fall?

Your family's life without you will be different and there are several changes you might take some time to ponder. If there is only one breadwinner in the family, would the surviving parent go to work if left to cope alone? If he or she did, how easily could a job be found; and how much could that parent expect to earn? If that parent does return to work, there will be certain obvious expenses, such as child care and the transportation cost of getting to and from work, and you can also expect your family to eat more of their meals in restaurants. People who work outside the home often need more new clothes than those who don't. Finally, your family will still need a vacation – a pleasure that is often beyond the reach of a single parent. Add to the monthly expenses one-twelfth of the annual amount you usually spend on your vacations.

The next factor to consider is the number of years your family will need an income from the insurance benefit. That will probably be at least the number of years until your youngest child is twenty-one or twenty-two years old. The final factor to consider is the effect of inflation. Although no one knows what the rate of inflation will be in the future, you can conservatively expect your family's investments to earn 3 percent more than the rate of inflation. That is the assumption we have made in the inflation factor table that you'll use to calculate your family's needs in the planning worksheet. Don't forget that income earned by investments is taxable so allow for this. (And don't think inflation in Canada is licked for good; it's just licked for now.)

Also, the table showing required investment capital is calculated assuming you will use the capital as well as the income; when the time period you have selected is over, all the money will be used up.

Once you've completed the worksheet – and you've discovered you need to buy insurance – your next step will be to determine the kind of life insurance policy you should buy. At first glance, this might seem the most painful task of all: There are 148 life insurance companies in Canada, many of them offering a full range of policies. You'll soon see that you can quickly narrow the choice down to just a few policies that are practical, desirable and affordable. Whatever your choice, make sure there will be enough death benefit to protect your family

And remember, this need will change. For many people, the need for life insurance is highest when their children are young and their mortgages high, with the family income not yet at its peak. The need for insurance will often decline as the children grow up, the mortgages are paid off, salaries increase and investments bear fruit. Although this is the norm, it's not necessarily so. A child or spouse could suffer a disabling illness or accident, you could decide to launch a family business or your family's steadily rising income could lead to a richer lifestyle. There are people whose lives are a series of moves into ever larger homes, with ever larger mortgages; their life insurance needs remain steady or even grow.

Because needs vary from family to family, and within the same family at different stages of its growth, it is not wise to buy life insurance and forget about it. Like a will, life insurance should be reviewed every time there is a significant change in your life, such as the birth of a child or the purchase of a new house, and at least every three years.

CHAPTER 3

The Basic Kinds of Life Insurance

IN SOME WAYS, SHOPPING for life insurance is like shopping for a new car. The major difference is that even the most unsophisticated shopper can look at a Ferrari and know that it's nice but hardly the car for a middle-class family with a modest income. And we all know that if a salesman tries to sell us a Lada for $50,000, it's not worth the price. With life insurance, however, most people can't tell at a glance if a given policy suits their needs or if it is good value for the premium.

The confusion isn't necessary. Like cars, life insurance policies have only a few key elements. Once understood, these can be used to compare one policy against another just as you might compare a mid-size family car made by General Motors with a mid-size family car made by Ford.

Almost all policies fall into one of two categories: term insurance and permanent insurance. Term insurance provides insurance protection only for an established period of time or to a particular age. Permanent insurance, as the name suggests, is in force until death. There are only three other elements that you must look at when comparing policies. These are:

The face amount or death benefit. This is the amount of money that will be paid to the beneficiary if the policyholder dies while the insurance is in force. The death benefit usually remains stable for the life of the policy but you can buy policies with death benefits that rise or fall.

The premium or cost of your insurance. The premiums on term policies usually rise over the years as the risk of your death rises. The premium can be guaranteed or negotiable. If it's negotiable, the premium may change at the insurance company's whim; if it's guaranteed, your premium will still rise every time you renew but it will be at a rate published and guaranteed in your policy. The premium on a permanent policy is usually fixed over the life of the policy or for a certain period of years; it will be more expensive than term insurance when you're young but less expensive in later years. However, some permanent policies allow you to vary your premiums from year to year depending on your ability, or desire, to pay.

The structure. Insurance would be a snap if you concerned yourself only with the protection and the cost. The "structure" of a life insurance policy lies in the riders, dividends, and pool of investments called the reserve. The riders are the bells and whistles you can add to your policy. Some riders boost the protection provided by your policy: the accidental-death rider, or double indemnity clause, will increase the death benefit paid to your beneficiaries if you die in an accident. Other riders protect your policy: with a waiver-of-premium rider you won't have to pay your premiums if you become disabled.

The pool of investments that builds in a permanent life insurance policy is called the reserve. The part of the reserve that can be refunded if the policy is cancelled is called the cash value. You can also borrow against the cash value. Some policies are "participating" policies; the owners of these policies receive regular payments called "dividends." These dividends are a return of some of the overpayment of premium during the year.

Basic term policies

Term policies are available with terms of one, five, or ten years or for as long as to age eighty. When the term is over, the life insurance coverage ends unless you renew it. If the policy is guaranteed renewable, the company cannot refuse to renew your insurance even if there has been a change in your health or occupation. However, the cost of the renewed insurance can be guaranteed or negotiable. If it is guaranteed, the company will have to renew your insurance at the premium published in the policy. The premium will be higher to reflect the increased possibility of death that comes naturally with age but it will not reflect a heart attack you might have had or a career switch from accountant to stunt pilot. If the policy is not guaranteed, the company may be free to charge any premium it wants – or a premium based on new interest rates, changes in general mortality assumptions, or changes in administrative costs or profit objectives.

A term policy's death benefits – the money that will be paid to your beneficiary if you die – can be level, increasing or decreasing. Usually the face value of a policy remains steady throughout the life of the policy while the premiums gradually rise. With a decreasing term policy, the premium is level but the face amount decreases. Decreasing term is seldom sold today except as mortgage insurance and is rarely competitively priced.

A term policy is usually, but not always, convertible. A conversion clause gives you the right to convert a term policy into a permanent policy without a medical examination. Although you might not need permanent insurance when you're young, the unfolding of your life is unpredictable. By the time you're fifty or fifty-five years old, you might have become so successful that your family is financially secure. You won't need term insurance to create a stream of income to protect your family; however, you might need insurance to pay the capital gains tax that will arise at your death because of the "deemed disposition" of your assets. This tax can be a damaging burden, especially if you're the owner of a family business. If you don't want your family to sell real estate or securities or family treasures to raise the cash needed to pay the taxes, you can cover this final tax bill with a permanent insurance policy.

Term insurance usually expires at age sixty-five or seventy – almost always before your actuarial life expectancy – making it unsuitable for estate planning. If you develop some heart trouble, high blood pressure, or diabetes, you might not be able to buy a permanent policy at standard rates, if at all. A conversion option would permit you to exchange your term policy for a permanent policy, with the same health status as when you purchased your original policy. The premium, however, would depend on the age at which you convert, not the age at which you bought the original term policy.

A common term policy would be guaranteed, five-year, renewable, and convertible. That means the premiums would increase every five years according to a schedule guaranteed in the contract. The company would guarantee to renew the policy every five years, typically to age seventy or seventy-five, and would offer to convert it into a permanent policy without evidence of insurability, often to age seventy, usually to age sixty-five. An important thing to remember is that most term insurance policies are designed to expire before you reach your actuarial life expectancy. In themselves, they are protection against premature death only.

Basic permanent insurance

Permanent insurance is much more complicated; and it has become more complicated with the recent development of new policies. The traditional permanent insurance was the whole life policy. With most whole life policies, the annual premium remains the same throughout the life of the policy. This makes the annual cost of the policy high when you're young, and the risk of death is low, but relatively inexpensive in later years when the risk of death is high. The payments beyond the cost of the pure insurance in the early years are held in reserve to be used by the insurance company to fund the policy at the later, more expensive ages. If you cancel the policy before death, some of this reserve might be refunded to you, since it is no longer needed by the insurance company. This refund is referred to as a "cash value" and a cash-value schedule would be listed in the policy if it is available. You cannot withdraw the cash from a whole life policy unless you cancel it. However, you can borrow against it at an interest rate that is established by the insurance company (usually near prime bank lending rates).

The cash value of a whole life policy exists for the protection of the policy owner. If you no longer need the policy or you decide you have made a mistake in purchasing it, you will receive a refund of at least some of your premiums if you have owned it for several years. The cash value is a safety net, like a parachute. Usually when you take a parachute on an airplane you don't expect to have to use it (unless you're a skydiver). Neither should you buy a whole life policy expecting to cancel it. If you should encounter a financial emergency, you will be able to borrow against the cash value. If your insurance needs change and you decide to cancel the policy after a few years, you will get some of your money back. But you will suffer a significant loss. A whole life policy's cash value does not benefit the beneficiaries. If you should die, your beneficiaries receive only the face amount of the policy; they do not receive any of the cash value, no matter how much there might be in the policy. In fact, if you have borrowed against the cash value, the money owed will be deducted from the death benefit.

The "whole life" policy derived its name from the fact that it protected you for "your whole life." (It could also have been called "until death" but would have been difficult to sell.) In the early days, policies did not have any cash value; if the policy was cancelled, the insurance company kept the reserve. Early in this century, consumers began to protest that this was unfair; laws were passed to force the insurance companies to return a portion of the reserve. An enterprising salesman began to tell consumers that this cash value was really "savings" and soon every whole life policy had a cash value. Some companies even increased the premiums, thereby boosting the cash value, to make the policies seem more appealing.

Variations on a theme

Buyers of whole life policies were left dissatisfied in two ways:

1. Sometimes they needed whole life insurance but were convinced that they would never cancel their policies. They didn't want to fund a cash value they would never claim.

2. The reserve of money that the industry called the policy owners' "savings" was owned and controlled by the insurance company. The owner had no say in the investment of the money or the returns, which were much less than could be made on other types of investments. If the insurance company did reap healthy returns on its reserves, the policy owners did not share in the windfall.

The life insurance industry responded with three very different policies: term-to-100, universal life and new money policies.

Term-to-100 insurance was first sold in Canada in 1979 by MoNY Life of Canada, which later merged with Halifax Life to become NN Life Insurance Co. of Canada. MoNY called its policy PermaTerm; the industry dubbed it term-to-100 because, like term insurance, it was uncluttered with cash values and, unlike whole life insurance, you continued to pay premiums until you were one hundred years old. Gradually the industry began to backtrack, adding cash values to make the policies more appealing. Sound like whole life? The confusion would be eliminated if the industry used the name "term-to-100" for any permanent policy that does not have a cash value and "whole life" for a policy with a cash value. This is the distinction a few in the industry have begun to adopt and the one we will use throughout this book.

Universal life insurance is a term insurance policy combined with a savings program. It, too, sounds like whole life but, unlike whole life, the insurance and savings are kept distinct (the insurance industry calls it "unbundled"). It's the industry's answer to the buy-term-invest-the-rest argument; you can build a pool of savings that is allowed to grow tax-free until it's taken out of the policy. While in the policy the savings are used to pay the actual premiums, thus conferring a tax benefit on the owner (pretax investment earnings pay the premium). You can decide how much insurance you want by increasing or decreasing the face amount of term insurance held by the policy. You can decide the premiums you want to pay, and for how long. You decide how you want the reserve invested; you can even withdraw cash from the reserve, not just borrow it, because it belongs to you and not to the insurance company, as is the case with whole life.

New money policies were launched in Canada by The Maritime Life Assurance Company in 1976 when consumers objected to the cautious projections of the insurance companies. At the time, the rate of return on insurance company investment portfolios (some of them invested in 1932 government bonds at 4 percent) hovered around 7 percent. Yet the prevailing market rates were closer to 11 percent. Maritime agreed to issue policies with premiums that reflected the higher returns on "new money" coming into the company – but warned the policy buyers that the policy would be adjusted every few years to reflect prevailing interest rates. If interest rates continued to climb, the premiums on the policy would drop – or the face value increase. If interest rates dropped, the policyholder would have a choice of paying higher premiums, accepting a lower face value, or choosing a combination of the two. Sharing the reward was balanced by sharing the risks as well.

The concept of "new money" is most common in term-to-100 insurance and whole life policies. In some of these policies, the insurance company will also adjust the cash value or paid-up value, two concepts we'll discuss in depth in chapter five.

"Par" policies and dividends

A second difference between life insurance policies – particularly whole life but also some term plans – is whether they pay dividends. Life insurance dividends are very different from the dividends you might receive from a company stock. Dividends from a stock investment are a share in the company's profits. Dividends from a participating life insurance policy are a partial refund of overpayment of premiums.

Life insurance actuaries, the number-crunchers who calculate insurance risks and set premiums, can predict very accurately how many people of a particular age will die in a year. But apart from mortality, they fare no better as forecasters than weathermen or economists. When setting the premium for their policies, the company must make conservative assumptions in order to guarantee that it will be able to meet its obligations and make a profit. On the other hand, as consumers we would not like to see the company make huge windfall profits if interest rates soar or if mortality improves dramatically.

Enter the participating policy. All insurance policies are priced to err on the side of the company – this gives the company a cushion. On a non-par policy, once the policy is sold, the premium is set and the company has to accept the risk of lower profit. On a par policy, the cushion is deliberately fatter – with the premiums higher than for a similar non-par policy. In fact, the premium is so high that you can reasonably expect a surplus to be declared each year, and a "dividend" paid out. Although the name – participating policy – arises from the phrase "participating in profits" the so-called profits are the surplus created by the overcharge in premiums. A life insurance policy that doesn't offer dividends is called a "non-par" policy.

Most par policies are sold by mutual insurance companies. Mutual companies are owned by the policy owners; the mere act of buying a life insurance contract from one of these firms makes you one of the owners of the company. In theory, the companies are run for the benefit of the policy owners; the insurance should represent the best value, since the company is "not-for-profit," and you should pay no more for your insurance than its actual cost. In reality, this is rarely true. (Always make sure you're paying a fair price for your insurance by shopping around.)

Mutual companies use part of their premium and investment income to fund special reserves, "for safety." These reserves are not returned to policyholders who die or cancel policies. Like a barrier reef in the sea, a mutual company owes its existence to the thousands who have left a legacy.

Of the 148 life insurance companies in Canada, about thirty are mutual companies. The rest are stock companies owned by shareholders. Many of the stock companies in Canada are owned by foreign insurance companies or foreign conglomerates.

How life insurance policies are priced

Whether you die the day after you take out your policy or many years later, your beneficiary is guaranteed the death benefit, as long as your policy is kept in force. That's the beauty of insurance. It transfers financial risk from someone who can't afford it – you – to a company that not only can afford it, but has planned for it. The price of shouldering that risk – the premium you pay each year – is based on several factors.

Contemplating mortality

Every type of insurance works on the idea that insurance companies can predict mishaps – houses are burgled and cars bumped and bicycles stolen and people die with predictable frequency within any particular group. Life insurance companies can then make sure that the premiums they collect will create a pool of funds from which they can meet any claim from their policyholders. Covering these claims is the primary expense of insurance companies. The actuaries spend hours forecasting as accurately as possible the rate of death among the policyholders in a given year. These forecasts are made in deaths per 1,000 lives insured for each age group. They might forecast that there will be 0.68 deaths for each 1,000 policyholders aged forty; 2.50 among its fifty-five-year-old policyholders.

These statistics are then used to determine how much $1,000 of life insurance should cost. If a forty-year-old man in average health for his age has a rating of 0.68, he will be charged $0.68 a year for each $1,000 of coverage for a year just to cover the mortality charge. A group of 100,000 forty-year-old men, each of average health, covered by $100,000 of life insurance, would each pay $68 in premiums. The company is predicting that sixty-eight of them will die that year, and it will have collected the $6,800,000 needed to cover the death benefits. (Note this is the cost of mortality, not the cost of the policy. A five-year renewable term policy, for a forty-year-old, male non-smoker would cost about $200 a year; $50 to $100 of that would pay the annual administration fee.)

Underwriting the risk

These mortality numbers differ from company to company as each screens and picks its own clients through its underwriting standards. Underwriting is the process that classifies you by risk; you will be a select, super-select, standard or substandard risk depending on a variety of factors. These factors will tell the insurance company whether the chances of your death are higher, lower, or about the same as others in your age group. The factors looked at are:

Your health. The life insurance companies try to avoid people who have health problems that increase their statistical likelihood of dying, and thus cost the company a death benefit sooner rather than later. Often you'll just be asked to answer a few questions about your health and medical history. The insurance companies have strict standards for weight and blood pressure and can insist that you take a medical examination, complete with an electrocardiogram and analysis of your blood and urine. The likelihood of having to undergo a medical increases with your age and the amount of coverage you're trying to buy.

Your work. If your work is dangerous, you will probably have to pay a higher premium.

Your lifestyle. Dangerous hobbies and habits also trigger higher premiums; smokers, especially, can expect to pay about twice as much for insurance as non-smokers.

Many people are a select risk but close to 10 percent qualify for super-select rates available from only a few companies. You don't have to be a marathon swimmer or an athlete; you do have to have a clean health record and good blood pressure. You also have to be slim and you cannot smoke, not even a pipe or cigar. Qualifying as super-select will earn you a discount of about 5 percent on your premiums.

Sometimes the underwriting standards are less strict. Some group insurance plans accept everyone who applies, no questions asked, although there are limits on the amount of coverage allowed. The anticipated mortality cost for this group of clients will be much higher than for people who have to answer questions about their health and personal habits. This is why group insurance is seldom cheaper.

The costs of doing business

You can't buy insurance just for the mortality charge. The companies have other costs, even if they aren't in business to make profits. They have to pay for the medical you take, the salaries of their staff, rent or maintenance for their offices, commissions to the agent or broker who sells you the policy and provides future service. Some companies have branch offices in virtually every town in Canada, elaborate recruiting and training programs, and a network of agents. Others depend on independent sales representatives and have only one head office. No matter what the administrative arrangement, the overheads are factored into the cost of insurance policies.

The impact of interest rates

When an insurance company sells a term-to-100 or whole life policy, it expects to collect premiums for twenty or thirty years and pay most of the death benefits in the last few of those years. The cost of paying those benefits will be covered not only by the premiums paid by the policyholders but also by the returns earned on the premiums invested. This rate of return is one of the factors that determines the cost of any long-term policy; the more conservative the anticipated earnings, the higher the premium charged the policyholder.

Let's look at an example – a forty-year-old man, who has just passed a rigorous examination of health, health history and lifestyle. This fine specimen has an average life expectancy to age seventy-three. If he buys a permanent policy, the insurance company will be collecting premiums for around thirty-two years before it pays the death claim. All of the premiums collected in the first three years will go to pay for the medical, the salesperson's commission, and all issuing costs. Thereafter, the company will need about 5 percent of future premiums to pay the annual administration costs. Starting with the fourth year, we'll assume the rest of the premium will be deposited in the reserve account, which is building up to pay for the eventual death benefit.

We'll start by calculating the absolute minimum annual premium that will fund a $500,000 death benefit at age seventy-two for this forty-year-old man. If it expects to earn a 3 percent return on the money it invests, the company must charge a premium of $11,300, at 5 percent it must charge $8,040, at 7 percent $5,630, at 9 percent $3,890, at 11 percent $2,660, and at 13 percent only $1,800 a year.

From this it is obvious that even small differences in the earnings assumption make a vast difference in the premiums that must be paid. In fact, the major risk in a guaranteed-premium policy is interest-rate fluctuation, not death. Although insurance companies don't know who will die each year, the rate of mortality can be very accurately predicted.

One of the most expensive $500,000 policies available in Canada in mid-summer 1994 for a healthy, non-smoking forty-year-old had a premium of $8,865 a year. If we assume that the company covers its issuing costs in the first two years and invests the premiums at 7 percent, it will have built a reserve of $506,871 by the time the policyholder is sixty-five. If the insured lives beyond age 65, or if interest rates exceed 7 percent, the policy will be very profitable for the company. At age sixty-five, the owner would get back only $220,500 if he cashed it in. This could trigger a quarter-million-dollar windfall for the company, since it keeps the balance of the reserve. One of the cheapest $500,000 whole life policies this man could have bought had a premium of $2,345 a year. If we make the same assumptions, this policy would have a reserve of only $130,079 by the time he reaches age sixty-five. The company would not amass a $500,000 reserve until he reached age 82. The first company will have no problem meeting its claim obligations, but the second must have made more aggressive assumptions than we did; the accumulated reserve would not be enough to pay the death benefit. The company must have assumed one of the following:

1. A higher rate of return. An 11 percent average return would be required to have the reserves break even at age seventy-two.

2. A longer life expectancy. The policy owners of the second company would have to live to age eighty-two for the policy to break even at 7 percent.

3. Lower initial and annual costs. If the company had no administrative or sales costs at all, the break-even age would be eighty.

4. Cancellation of many of the policies before death. The company could use the surplus reserves of the lapsed policies to subsidize the benefits paid by the remaining policies.

In fact, the second company probably assumed a combination of lower costs, longer life expectancy, lapse subsidies, and higher earnings.

Why life insurance is a bargain

In round numbers, term life insurance in Canada sells for double the cost of mortality. This makes it about the cheapest in the world. In addition, and unlike term insurance sold in the United States, Canadian term insurance usually guarantees all future renewal rates.

We enjoy low prices for three major reasons. First, the health and life expectancy of Canadians is better than average. We are an affluent country, with national medical care. Second, the insurance companies invest their premiums until required to pay claims, and the earnings generated for the companies by our traditionally higher interest rates reduce the premiums that must be collected to fund benefits. Third, Canadian life insurance companies invest more heavily in stocks and real estate than their American counterparts; and historically stocks and real estate have done especially well over the long term.

CHAPTER 4

Term Insurance

THERE ARE MANY KINDS OF term insurance policies but the differences lie in length of time the coverage lasts, whether or not you have the right to renew the policy, and the guarantees on the future premiums. All of these details will be set out in your life insurance contract.

Reading your life insurance contract

Not all insurance contracts are the same. There are common provisions, however. In this chapter we'll cover the typical elements that you'll find in virtually every life insurance policy, whether term or permanent. In chapter five, we'll cover the provisions peculiar only to permanent insurance.

The front page of every life policy sets out the relevant details. It lists:

• The name of the person whose life is insured.

• The issue date of the policy.

• The policy owner, who is not necessarily the person insured. Many executives and other key people are insured by their companies. Business partners often insure each other, and sometimes spouses own the policy on their mate as part of an estate plan.

• The type of insurance bought.

• The face amount of the policy.

• The premium. The premium will either be guaranteed for the duration of the contract or future premiums will not be guaranteed at all. Unless the policy states otherwise, they are fixed and guaranteed. (This information is sometimes found on a schedule in the policy.)

The only personal detail that might be missing on the front page is the name of the beneficiary – the person or persons, company, organization, or charity that will receive the money if you die. Many companies don't list the beneficiary on the front page of the policy because it could eventually be misleading. The choice of beneficiary is the right of the policy owner, who can change the beneficiary at any time, unless there is an "irrevocable" beneficiary. The beneficiary is usually listed later in the contract; if the application is reproduced at the back of the policy, it will contain the names of the original beneficiaries. Or, it could be amended by subsequent election.

The beneficiary

Although married couples usually name each other the beneficiary of their insurance policies, this could leave their estates exposed to legal and financial problems. If they were to die together in an accident, the insurance benefits could be paid to the estate. Since the estate will be responsible for paying all debts, including income taxes, and could be involved in a lawsuit, perhaps even a lawsuit arising from the accident that caused the deaths, the result could be financial disaster. The money would be tied up for years and be of no use to those whom it was supposed to benefit, such as the children.

Whenever the named beneficiary is a living individual – and not a company or business – there is always the risk that the beneficiary could die before the person insured. The solution is to name a "contingent" beneficiary. For a family, this would be the children. An insurance application would read something like this: Beneficiary: Valerie Smith, wife; Contingent Beneficiary: Ann Smith and Jennifer Smith, children of the insured.

Insurance companies always ask for the relationship of the beneficiaries to the insured. They want to be sure there is an "insurable interest." Insurers insist there be a legitimate need for the insurance, that it be paid to the appropriate person, and that the amount of insurance is not excessive. You cannot insure your Uncle Fred, naming yourself as beneficiary, just because you think he's a terrible driver and bound to kill himself. You would not be able to show the insurable interest, a financial loss to yourself if Fred were to die.

Beneficiaries should be aware that they can take steps to make sure that they will remain the policy beneficiary. The insurance company can accept the appointment of the beneficiary as "irrevocable." This must be done by the policy owner and any future change in beneficiary or any change in the death benefit would have to be approved by the existing beneficiary.

The term of the policy

Although your premiums are paid annually, each policy must make it clear for how long it will remain in force. It will either state a specific number of years, such as five, ten, twenty, or to age sixty-five. A permanent policy will state "for the life of the insured."

The renewal clause

"Renewable" means that the policy can be renewed for another term without evidence of insurability – that is, without a medical examination. By simply writing a cheque for the new premium, you are able to keep the insurance in force regardless of health, occupation, or avocation. If you must answer any questions to requalify for the insurance, the policy is not guaranteed renewable.

A few term policies do not contain a guaranteed right of renewal. If a consumer was required by a bank to post life insurance to secure a loan, a non-renewable policy matching the term of the loan might be the cheapest way to do it. In practice, for a little more (usually only 1 percent), the policy can be made renewable. This would give the insured the right to renew the policy for another term – at a higher premium, of course. You should consider guaranteed renewability a must. You might renegotiate the loan for a longer term; or a health problem, such as a heart attack, might make it advisable to keep the insurance in force.

The table of renewal premiums

The insurance company should not only guarantee your right of renewal; it should also guarantee the future cost of your insurance. Dramatic changes in mortality and interest rates, or even taxation of the insurance company, do not give the company the right to change the premium or benefits of a guaranteed policy. Your premiums will rise in step with the risk of death; however, the rate at which your premiums will rise should be guaranteed in the policy. If the renewal rates are not guaranteed, you could be exposed to a huge unexpected rise in your insurance costs.

Some companies issue guaranteed renewable term policies, and offer a second set of "preferred" renewal rates that are cheaper than the guaranteed rates. To qualify for these "preferred" rates, the insured must pass a medical and answer questions about work and sports activities at renewal. About a third of the term policies offered include such "renewal underwriting." Such policies are not

A Comparison of Preferred and Guaranteed Renewal Rates

$500,000 5-year term
Male, age 50, non-smoker

| Age | Mutual Life Assurance | | Transamerica Life |
	Preferred	Maximum	Guaranteed
50		$1,820	$1,665
55	$2,975	5,760	2,755
60	5,420	10,570	4,315
65	8,385	16,375	7,885
70	13,365	26,155	15,625
75	NA	NA	23,280

SOURCE: COMPULIFE SOFTWARE INC.   AUGUST 1995

TABLE II

recommended, since you can usually find a policy with completely guaranteed renewal rates for a price similar to the preferred rates.

As you can see in Table II, the guaranteed renewal rates for a $500,000 five-year policy for a non-smoking fifty-year-old male are about the same as the preferred rates from another company. If this man was unable to qualify for those preferred rates at age-60 renewal, his premiums would jump by almost $7,600 a year rather than $1,510.

The conversion clause

Term policies are usually "convertible." This means they can be changed to a permanent policy without medical evidence of insurability. We've discussed the reasons why a conversion clause is necessary in chapter one but we'd like to emphasize its importance here. It is possible that as you build your wealth, your family worth may become significant enough to trigger a heavy capital gains tax at your death, especially if you own a family business.

The ability to convert a policy also becomes important if you develop a health problem and become uninsurable, or at least not insurable at a standard premium. Yet you might need permanent insurance to cover capital gains taxes at your death, especially if you are able to build significant wealth or a healthy family business over your lifetime. On the other hand, if you suffer any one of a variety of diseases or accidents, it could disrupt your income, life expectancy and insurability. Your ability to save and invest for retirement could be reduced or even eliminated. In such circumstances, you might be forced to rely on your insurance to fund your husband or wife's retirement.

This is not an uncommon scenario; almost one-third of us will suffer a serious accident or illness before retirement. The original need for life insurance to create the estate we do not yet have changes to the need to create an estate we can no longer hope to build.

Although most term policies are convertible, there are restrictions. Usually you can convert only up to a certain age, often age sixty-five. Sometimes the choice of policies to which you can convert is limited; most companies sell term-to-100 but many do not make these policies available through conversion. They know that most people want to convert because of a change in their health, and the insurance company doesn't want them to buy an inexpensive policy. There's a very good chance that if you do eventually convert from term to permanent the company will have changed both the kind of policies to which you can convert and their cost. However, when pricing your term insurance you should also ask your agent or broker to look at the cost of the permanent insurance available through conversion when pricing your term insurance. Choose the company that is competitive in both markets. There is little point in having a conversion option if the ultimate insurance is going to be too expensive; making your choice on existing practices is the best you can do.

Dividends

The contract will simply say this policy participates in the profits of the company if it is a par policy, or that it does not if it is a non-par policy. There will be no guarantees or information on the company's history of paying dividends.

Suicide

By law, every life insurance policy carries a clause stating that the policy will not pay the death benefit if the person insured commits suicide within two years of the issue of the policy. Not only does this protect the insurance companies; it discourages depressed individuals from seeing suicide and a new large life insurance benefit to their loved ones as a solution to their problems.

Death claims within the first two years of a policy will require a statement from the attending physician, attesting that the death was from an identifiable cause other than suicide. Once the policy is over two years old, suicide is no longer grounds for denying the payment of benefits.

Finally, every policy will explain how the insurance benefit can be paid if you die. Usually, beneficiaries take the death benefit in cash. However, there are other choices. It can be held on deposit with the insurance company or converted to an annuity and paid out over a number of years.

While these choices are generally available to the beneficiary, the policy owner can also specify that a particular option must be used. For example, a parent of a mentally handicapped child might be reluctant to name the child as beneficiary for a cash benefit, finding it more practical to specify that the money be paid to the child as a monthly income for the rest of his or her life.

Making a claim is discussed in detail in chapter twenty-three.

CHAPTER 5

Whole Life Insurance and Its Hybrids

WHOLE LIFE INSURANCE IS THE traditional and still the most commonly sold kind of life insurance. Among the many whole life policies, the most common is straight life – your premiums and the death benefit paid by the policy continue for your whole life.

A variation on straight life is the policy that can be paid up before death. The ultimate is the single premium policy. Between payments until death and one very large premium is just about every duration of premium-paying period possible. The most common is twenty payments, called 20-pay-life policies, and payments-to-age-sixty-five. The stripped-down "whole life" insurance is term-to-100 policies. The more complex is universal life, which combines insurance with a pool of savings that are managed by the policy owner. This is discussed in chapter six.

Thus, permanent life insurance policies can be split into two groups: those that have cash values and those that do not. The provisions of the policies that make them so confusing are the cash values and options if you want to cancel the policy. Let's look at both in detail.

The surrender or "non-forfeiture" clauses

When you buy a permanent policy, your premiums are used to create a reserve that will grow to eventually fund the death benefit. If you decide to cancel the policy, you do not have to forfeit all of the reserve funds; you will have several choices for recovering something for the premiums you've paid. These are referred to as "non-forfeiture values" in the policy.

The cash value is the most commonly used non-forfeiture value; it's a return of some of the cash paid to the insurance company over the years. The buildup of cash value is different in every policy. The traditional whole life policy offers a cash value starting around the third year. However, there are whole life policies that will refund all of the premiums you've paid at the end of the first year. At the other end of the whole life spectrum are policies that offer a cash value on only one day of the entire life of the contract. This day is typically the anniversary of your purchase of the policy in the year you turn sixty-five or after twenty years, whichever is later. The later and more restricted the opportunity to claim a cash value, the lower the cost.

Choosing the cash value is not always the best way to wind up whole life insurance. Sometimes a policy is cancelled or premiums are unpaid because of financial stress, not because the policy is no longer needed or wanted. In these situations, the other non-forfeiture values could be of more interest. Instead of taking the cash, you could take a paid-up permanent policy with a lower death benefit or an extended term policy.

The reduced, paid-up benefit allows you to stop paying premiums yet keep a reduced amount of life insurance in force until death. The longer the whole life policy is in force, the larger the reduced paid-up benefit. The extended term option would keep the full amount of insurance in force but only for a specific number of years, months or days. This is a plausible option if the person insured is seriously ill with a terminal disease; the family will not want the policy to lapse or even be reduced. If the extended term period is longer than the reduced life expectancy of the insured, it is a perfect solution to the financial crisis the family might be facing.

Every whole life policy has a table that shows how much money or paid-up insurance would be available if you cancel your policy. Sometimes these values are given in rates per $1,000 of insurance, sometimes they are given as actual dollar amounts.

Surrendering a whole life insurance policy

The value of the options available to you if you decide to cancel your insurance will be illustrated in your policy. They're usually presented in a table with columns representing the cash value and paid-up insurance value. Sometimes these two values are presented in separate tables so that you do not confuse one with the other. The figures in Table III are the values that would build over time if the policy was bought by a forty-year-old non-smoking man. We've chosen two policies: the Guaranteed Annual Premium Plan by

Non-Forfeiture Options on Surrender of a Policy

This table illustrates the non-forfeiture values available to you should you decide to surrender a cash value policy. It illustrates the cash value and paid-up value of two different $500,000 policies sold to a forty-year-old man who is a non-smoker. The third non-forfeiture option is an extended term policy but the values are not published in the policy.

Years since the policy was issued	—Guaranteed annual premium—		————Growth protector————	
	Cash value	Paid-up value	Cash value	Paid-up value
5		$10,000		
10	$22,500	74,500	$1,000	$12,500
15	50,500	139,000	18,000	163,500
20	87,000	202,000	50,500	330,000
At age 65	125,500	249,000	107,500	516,500
At age 75	214,500	331,500	328,000	942,500

TABLE III

Zurich Life and the Growth Protector by Financial Life, to illustrate the wide differences between policies.

The insurance company does not pay income taxes on any of the interest earned in the reserve. However, if you cancel the policy and take the cash, you will have to pay income tax on most of the money you receive. Ask the agent to illustrate these cash values after tax. The taxable portion is determined under a complex formula but usually works out to about 75 percent of the total cash value, lower in the early years and increasing as time passes. The tax treatment of policies can vary dramatically, especially in equity investment options of universal life policies. Obtain the exact amount you will receive from the company before deciding to buy a policy or cancel an existing policy.

There are several good reasons for cancelling a policy: Perhaps you have sold your business and your family is no longer exposed to a potentially damaging tax burden, or maybe the beneficiary your insurance was to protect has died. Before you cancel and take the cash, ask your agent about converting the policy into an annuity. Not only might you earn an excellent investment return, you would be earning interest on money that would otherwise be lost in taxes. You will pay tax on some of the income received but, over time, your income tax bill will be lower.

Policy loans

You can usually borrow up to 90 percent of the cash value in your policy. Old policies issued before the early 1960s stipulate a maximum loan interest of 5 or 6 percent. Later policies allow the insurance companies to set the interest rate; usually, the rates are similar to prevailing bank lending rates. A policy loan is a private transaction that does not show up on your credit history. It would not, therefore, infringe on your credit limit at the bank. However, if you die with a policy loan outstanding, the money you owe will be deducted from the death benefit. Make sure that you do not endanger the financial security of the people your life insurance is intended to protect.

Premium-paying period

In most whole life policies you can decide whether you want to pay for your insurance over the life of the policy or in a much shorter period of time. This is much like paying a mortgage; the more quickly you pay it, the less it will cost. The premium-paying period could be seven years, ten years, fifteen years, twenty years, or longer. Choosing a shorter period increases your premiums, but might reduce the final cost. Ask your agent to do a present-value calculation for each of the premium-payment periods you are being offered. This will tell you how much you will be paying for the policy in today's dollars.

Again, make sure the calculations include all of the tax implications. Maritime Life created a flurry of actuarial activity in Canada when it introduced a single premium whole life policy in 1976. The premium was about seven times the typical annual premium for an ordinary whole life policy at the time. Maritime even offered to finance the purchase of the policy with an immediate policy loan. Agents enticed consumers with the phrase: "Pay us seven premiums, or pay them for the rest of your life!" Unfortunately, although this policy is still being sold, the cash value of a new policy is now taxable and the policy is no longer a good buy.

Term-to-100 policies

A term-to-100 policy is a stripped-down whole life policy. These policies build a reserve, just as a whole life policy does, but the funds are kept by the insurance company if the policy is cancelled. As a result, term-to-100 is usually less expensive than whole life. Premiums on term-to-100 policies are generally payable for life.

However, the premium-paying period could be shortened so that premiums stop at age sixty-five, or even sooner. Some term-to-100 policies also have paid-up values, though they are not usually as generous as those in a whole life policy. A $500,000 policy might become a paid-up $150,000 policy after twenty years; after twenty-five years of premiums it might become a paid-up $250,000 policy.

Universal life policies

Universal life insurance policies were first marketed in Canada in 1982. These policies usually combine one-year renewable term insurance with an investment fund within the policy. This investment fund is sheltered from taxes, but unlike the savings in a whole life policy, the savings in a universal life plan are owned and controlled by you, not the insurance company. This a life insurance product created by the industry for the investment-wise, tax-burdened consumer. This is a complex product yet you are not protected by any government body; unlike the securities industry, life insurance companies are not subject to disclosure rules requiring the release of all relevant information before a financial product is purchased. They are not obliged at the time of the presentation to disclose tax liabilities, premium guarantees, cash value yields, or face value guarantees. However, this may change as Ontario currently has draft legislation requiring agents to disclose, in writing, relevant policy information at the time of sale.

For this reason, we will devote the next chapter to a discussion of this more recent product. Our one piece of advice here is: Ask plenty of questions before you buy.

CHAPTER 6

Universal Life Insurance

THROUGHOUT THIS BOOK, WE stress the virtues of life insurance that is inexpensive, easy to understand, and easy to compare. Universal life, which is an investment as well as insurance, is none of these things. Yet for a well-heeled policyholder-investor who shops very carefully and chooses wisely, it often makes sense.

Before plunging into the nitty-gritty of universal life, let's step back for a moment. Since the risk of death increases with age, the cost of insuring someone against death goes up each year. Yet many policies have a level premium over a number of years, or for life. Insurance companies are able to set these premiums by charging more than necessary in the early years to build up a reserve fund that will cover the actual mortality costs in later years.

The premium of every level premium life insurance policy must be a compromise. Even a five-year term policy is an average of the cost of a series of one-year term rates. Ten, twenty, and term-to-sixty-five premiums are an average of the increasing annual cost of one-year term rates. Every policy of more than a year's protection must build a reserve; this reserve is invested by the insurance company. Thus the insurance companies must also predict interest rates and their rate of return on the reserves invested.

Universal life policies give special emphasis to these reserves, and place the management of the investments in your hands. Because you manage the reserve, you can also alter your premiums or the insurance coverage to suit your own needs. If you have another child you can increase your policy's death benefit, provided you are medically fit. If you come into extra money, you can make a large payment to the savings reserve and reduce your costs in coming years. (This is much like making a large prepayment on your mortgage.) The flexibility is tremendous, but the greater appeal of universal life policies is the ability it gives you to pay for your insurance premiums from a pool of investments sheltered from tax. If you're in the top marginal tax bracket, this can cut the actual cost of insurance in half.

Every universal life policy sets out a range of possible premiums. The minimum premium will build the reserve just enough to carry the policy through to age 100. The maximum premium deliberately builds far more in the reserve than necessary. This reserve is allowed to accumulate interest (or capital gains if you choose an equity investment) without triggering an income tax liability. Thus, the policy reserve becomes a tax shelter for building savings, not unlike savings in an RRSP although the contributions are not deductible.

The Income Tax Act has a formula for defining the maximum policy reserve permitted before a contract is considered a taxable investment rather than a tax-deferred life insurance policy. Without this legal constraint, there would be nothing to stop a life company from merging a $1 million guaranteed investment certificate or term deposit with a $1,000 life policy, calling the package a "life policy," and selling it as a tax shelter.

Current rules are fairly generous. For example, a forty-year-old can buy a $500,000 permanent policy for as little as $2,275 a year; but a universal life policy will permit an annual premium as high as $12,331. This would shelter more than $10,000 a year in "surplus" reserves. The reserve in a universal life policy is a savings account owned by you. It can be added to, or withdrawn from, without upsetting the life insurance — the money belongs to you, not to the insurance company. Premiums can even be skipped as long as there is enough money in the reserve account to pay the mortality costs and management fees. This makes universal life significantly different from whole life, where the cash values belong to the insurance company and are available only if you borrow the money or cancel the policy.

We never used to recommend life insurance as an investment. But as non-RRSP tax shelters, especially good ones, became rare, universal life insurance has emerged, almost by default, as one of the better opportunities. There are pitfalls that we'll discuss later.

The investment component

Most universal policies offer a variety of investments. Policyholders can choose between daily interest savings accounts, guaranteed investment certificates, and mutual fund investments in stocks, bonds

A Comparison of Universal Life and Term-to-100

This table compares the pool of funds available to you or your family if you purchase universal life against the funds that would be available if you purchase term-to-100 and invest the difference in premiums in GICs or equity mutual funds. It looks at those values in two circumstances: if the policies are surrendered at age seventy and if you die at age seventy with the life insurance still in force. Based on a marginal tax rate of 40%, life insurance face amount of $500,000, and $10,170 available to invest for ten years starting at age forty.

| | Pool of savings if surrendered | | Death benefit at age 70 | |
	Before tax	After tax	Before tax	After tax
Term-to-100 + GICs	$ 581,804	$ 292,428	$1,081,804	$792,428
Universal life incl GICs	690,392	415,997	1,190,392	1,190,392
Term-to-100 + fund	1,199,459	839,621	1,699,459	1,339,621
Universal life incl fund	1,408,577	845,146	1,908,577	1,908,577

TABLE IV

and mortgages. The investments may be merged with the insurance company's own reserves, or they may be held separately in segregated funds. Using the example of a forty-year-old, non-smoking man buying a $500,000 policy, let's look at the tax advantages of buying a universal life policy. This policy would allow him to deposit up to $12,331 in the tax-sheltered reserve, stopping the deposits after ten years. A term-to-100 policy within the universal life plan would cost $2,161 a year, leaving him with $10,170 a year to invest for ten years. If the investments earned 7 percent a year, and were taxed at 40 percent, his investment pool would build to $292,428 by the time he reached age seventy.

The universal life policy, on the other hand, would have accumulated $690,392 in policy reserves by age seventy. That's $397,964 more than an unsheltered investment. If he died at this age, this money ($690,392) would be paid to his beneficiaries tax-free, in addition to the $500,000 of life insurance that both policies would pay. If he withdrew the money in the universal insurance policy before his death, he would have to pay about $274,395 in taxes, leaving him with about $415,997 in his pocket (if he paid tax at a rate of 40 percent). The universal life policies would leave his family $123,569 richer than the term-to-100 – if he invests in a GIC or term deposit also yielding 7 percent.

The result would be very different if he invests in an equity mutual fund. The $10,170-a-year savings would build over the years without triggering a tax bill every year. If the return from the mutual fund was 10 percent a year, he would have $1,199,459 by the time he reached age seventy. If the fund investment was sold and the capital gains tax paid, he would have $839,621 in his pocket. If he died, and capital gains tax was not triggered, his family would have the entire $1,199,459 plus $500,000 insurance or $1,699,459 – $509,067 more than from the universal life policy. If his death did trigger a capital gains tax, his family would receive only $1,339,621 from the investments (and $500,000 from the insurance) or $149,229 more than they would receive from the universal life policy.

However, the deposits to the universal life plan can also be invested in a mutual fund with a similar yield. Tax sheltered over the years, they could do even better. For example, if the investments in the universal life policy generated 10 percent and all the proceeds were paid out tax-free as a death benefit at age seventy, the amount paid out would be $1,908,577.

The major difference between a universal life policy and a combination of term-to-100 and a mutual fund is the impact on the insurance if the savings are withdrawn. The owner of the term-to-100 policy would continue to pay $2,275 each year to keep a $500,000 policy in force. The life insurance in a universal life policy, however, is sometimes annual renewable term, which becomes very expensive at older ages. At age seventy the annual premium could reach more than $20,000 and keep rising each year. This could be funded by leaving $300,000 on deposit in the policy. That way, the tax-sheltered interest earnings would pay for the future cost of the insurance. Any balance would be paid out at death.

It is the annually renewable term aspect that has made universal life uncertain for planning purposes. However, there is a growing trend among life insurers to permit the use of their guaranteed term-to-100 products. For example, if the cost of insurance and administration is fixed at $2,161 to age 100, we have rather different values. $10,170 is then available to invest and, at 7 percent, this will compound to $690,392 by age seventy (using the same example).

Since it's term-to-100, the mortality and expense charge is still only $2,161 annually so only about $31,000 needs to be left in the reserve to cover expenses. This leaves the rest to grow free of tax and eventually provide a retirement income – which will be taxed as it is received unless it is received as a tax-free death benefit.

It is important to remember that, unlike the minimum withdrawal requirements on a RRIF, there aren't any rules regarding the amounts you must withdraw from a universal life contract. You can take out what you want, pay tax on it, and leave the rest in the shelter for tax-free passage to your beneficiary.

The strength of the universal life policy lies in its tax advantages; these advantages are far greater for anyone in a high tax bracket but not as significant if you're in a low- or middle-income tax bracket. Any comparison between a universal life policy and a term-to-100 policy has to take into account the after-tax results if you die or if you claim your investments while alive.

The concept of universal life is good. However, by mixing life insurance and investments, the complexity of shopping and comparing is multiplied. You have to choose with great care: Unlike the flexibility in switching an RRSP, once you've purchased a universal life policy, you cannot change plans without incurring a tax on all the interest or gains accumulated. There is also a possibility that you may not be insurable at a later date, so choose carefully.

The insurance component

The insurance part of the contract is usually a form of term insurance, with the premium debited against the reserve account each year. You would be wise to have a base of term-to-100 with a top-up of annual or ten-year term if required. Since term insurance is cheap in the early years, the investment pool (reserve) builds very quickly in the early years of the policy. The face value of that insurance can vary from year to year. In most policies, you can choose to have the reserve paid at your death to your beneficiaries on top of the face amount of the insurance coverage. The advantage for the policyholder is that the "savings" are paid tax-free as a life insurance death benefit.

Some universal policies use a two-tier life premium table. These policies quote low premiums, which they state they hope to be able to use indefinitely, but also quote a guaranteed maximum that cannot be exceeded. Some companies offer term-to-100 insurance: This is a much more attractive choice if you intend to withdraw your funds and keep the insurance. Never buy a universal policy without a guaranteed top-end premium valid for the life of the contract. They cost a bit more but they offer the most security.

The administration fees

When analyzing the merits of universal life policies as an investment, keep in mind that a 2 percent premium tax will be deducted. There will also be surrender charges if you cash the policy within a certain period of time — usually around fourteen years. Finally, you must consider the annual administration and management fees, since some policies charge much more than others. And even if the initial administration charge is low, it may not be guaranteed to stay that way. The insurance company might have the right to increase the charges. Look for a plan that specifies and guarantees the administration charges, or at least includes a top-end guarantee. The company will send you an annual statement telling you what percentage of your premiums went to cover the company's management fees, the mortality charges, and the savings reserve.

Life insurance as an investment

Despite all the advice you've heard – in this book and elsewhere – about keeping investments and insurance separate, this chapter has introduced the concept that insurance-cum-investment can make sense, especially for high-bracket taxpayers, if the policy is chosen carefully. By the same token, some whole life policies that otherwise would be rejected out-of-hand because they are outrageously expensive can make sense if considered as a life-insured investment.

You have seen that universal life can work as an investment because the money that builds within the policy is either tax-deferred (until cash is withdrawn from the policy) or tax-exempt (if kept until death). Such a policy is what the life insurance industry calls "exempt." Almost all policies sold in Canada are "exempt" under tax law.

The Coopers & Lybrand Tax Planning Checklist, published by CCH Canadian Ltd., advises: "Those looking for tax shelters or deferral mechanisms may wish to explore the significant benefits that may be derived from an 'exempt' life insurance policy. While professional advice may be needed, it is to be noted that a substantial portion of the income from such investment accumulates free of tax, that such income can be utilized before death, and the proceeds are not subject to tax on death . . . such policies may be a powerful tool in the tax planning arsenal.

"While many people think of life insurance as pure protection, and would not consider it to be an investment, let alone a tax shelter, the general choking-off of most shelters and the anti-avoidance rules ought to convince many investors to look more favourably upon life insurance. . . . The returns from virtually tax-free accumulation after the deduction of insurance costs, compared to taxable accumulations, can be quite remarkable. . . . Those with capital to invest would be well advised not to overlook this important shelter [and eventual source of capital]."

We must stress that we are not discussing basic protection when we are talking about life insurance as an investment. Basic protection is the first priority and use of the tax-deferred savings vehicle, such as universal life for specific purposes, must be a lower priority in family financial planning. A few examples of such specific purposes might be helpful here. The important thing to remember is that there must be a life insurance component in order for the tax-free accumulation to take place.

For example, a policy could be purchased on the life of a parent to be given to the child after reaching age eighteen. Then the funds could be withdrawn to fund the child's education – or left in place if they are not needed. It costs about $6,800 a year to attend the University of British Columbia, including tuition, room and board. In nineteen years this could cost closer to $11,924, if we assume 3 percent inflation. For a child just born, the parents could invest $1,200 annually in a "self-completing" universal life educational plan. The plan is called self-completing since it includes a death benefit of $19,500 plus an accumulating account value. When the child is nineteen years old, $11,384 will be paid out each year indexed at 3 percent for four years to the child and taxed in the child's hands. (Table V illustrates the death benefit being on the child's father, who, in this example, is a thirty-year-old non-smoking man.)

In another example, a forty-year-old non-smoking man hopes to retire at age sixty-five. Although he makes his maximum RRSP contributions, he is still concerned that he won't have enough money to live comfortably when he retires. If he invests $2,501 in a universal life plan for twenty years the policy will have accumulated almost $130,000 by the time he is sixty-five years old. (It will also have an insurance death benefit of over $300,000.) If he invested $2,500 in GICs instead, he will have about $97,291 (we've assumed he earns 7 percent in both cases). If he withdraws $6,000 the first year (increas-

Insurance as Savings for Education

NN Financial: "The Educator Plus"
Contractual annual deposit: $300
Additional annual deposit: $900
Total annual deposit: $1,200

Age	Annual deposits	Account value	Withdrawals	Insurance protection
1	$1,200	$1,198	0	$20,698
2	1,200	2,480	0	21,980
3	1,200	3,852	0	23,352
4	1,200	5,320	0	24,820
5	1,200	6,890	0	26,390
6	1,200	8,570	0	28,070
7	1,200	10.368	0	29,868
8	1,200	12,292	0	31,792
9	1,200	14,351	0	33,851
10	1,200	16,554	0	36,054
11	1,200	18,911	0	38,411
12	1,200	21,432	0	40,932
13	1,200	24,131	0	43,631
14	1,200	27,018	0	46,518
15	1,200	30,107	0	49,607
16	1,200	33,413	0	52,913
17	1,200	36,950	0	56,450
18	1,200	40,735	0	60,235
19	0	32,091	$11,384	51,591
20	0	22,501	11,762	42,001
21	0	11,888	12,077	31,388
22	0		12,600	0

This table shows the wealth building in a universal life insurance policy to which a parent deposits $1,200 every year. The funds grow tax-free, earning 7% a year, and will be used to pay for a child's education beginning in the nineteenth year. The policy will provide life insurance on the parent's life should he or she die before the plan matures, ensuring funds will be in place for the child's school expenses.

TABLE V

ing his withdrawals by 3 percent a year with a tax rate of 40 percent on the earnings) the GIC account would run out of money at age eighty-one. The universal life plan would not only pay him an in-

Insurance as Investment

NN Life Insurance Company of Canada: Challenger
Insurance estate value at age 65: $128,173   Interest rate: 7%
GIC estate value at age 65: $97,291   40-year-old male, non-smoker

| Age | Guaranteed Investment Certificate | | The Challenger | |
	Income	Estate	Income	Estate
66	$6,000	$88,945	$6,000	$132,174
67	6,180	86,315	6,180	136,340
68	6,365	83,384	6,365	140,680
69	6,556	80,133	6,556	145,201
70	6,753	76,543	6,753	149,915
71	6,955	72,593	6,955	154,832
72	7,164	68,263	7,164	159,964
73	7,379	63,530	7,379	165,322
74	7,600	58,369	7,600	170,920
75	7,828	52,757	7,828	176,771
76	8,063	46,668	8,063	182,891
77	8,305	40,073	8,305	189,296
78	8,554	32,945	8,554	196,003
79	8,811	25,253	8,811	203,030
80	9,075	16,966	9,075	210,398
81	9,347	8,051	9,347	218,127
82	9,628	0	9,628	226,241
83	0	0	9,917	234,765
84	0	0	10,214	243,724
85	0	0	10,521	253,148
86	0	0	10,836	263,067
87	0	0	11,161	273,515
88	0	0	11,496	284,526
89	0	0	11,841	296,141
90	0	0	12,196	308,400
91	0	0	12,562	321,347
92	0	0	12,939	335,032
93	0	0	13,327	349,506
94	0	0	13,727	364,826
95	0	0	14,139	381,052
96	0	0	14,563	412,839
97	0	0	15,000	447,362
98	0	0	15,450	484,855
99	0	0	15,914	525,574
100	0	0	0	569,797

TABLE VI

dexed income until past age 100, the death benefit would have grown to more than $400,000.

Let's take a look at the same man at age forty (his daughter is now ten years old). He combines his family's life insurance needs, his need to fund his daughter's education, and his retirement savings into one universal life policy. He pays $10,565 annually for twenty years. This gives him a joint-first-to-die death benefit – a policy that will pay $500,000 when either he or his wife dies and provide $250,000 term insurance on his life for twenty years and $250,000 on his wife's life for ten years. It allows the same indexed withdrawals for his daughter's education and it provides an indexed income of $10,000 when he reaches age sixty-five – indexed and taxable but it will last until he reaches age 100. If he lives past this age he'll receive the death benefit of $1,000,000. The policy also contains a living benefit rider that will give him $25,000 if he is stricken with one of a number of dread diseases (see chapter thirteen). If his plans change he can take out more money (and pay tax on most of it) or he can leave it in place and have it pass tax-free to his beneficiary. He could never do the same thing with GICs; the cost of insurance would use up all of the $10,000 annual deposit (see Table VII).

A less recognized advantage of investment life insurance is the expertise that life insurance companies have developed in managing money. Many now offer mutual funds, extremely attractive investment alternatives, for the funds within a life insurance policy. The return from mutual funds can fluctuate but over time it can be much greater than you would receive from a guaranteed investment. (The tables in this chapter have all assumed a consistent 7 percent return on investment.)

Life insurance for investment purposes requires the expertise of an adviser familiar with insurance concepts, taxation and investing. As with most purchases of any financial product, you owe it to yourself to become familiar with the intricacies of the product, at least to some extent. Life insurance is still sold using a lot of smoke and mirrors; make sure you look past all the fast talk. You need to know what you are buying and why it will work for you. In fact, before you buy insist upon being shown a number of alternatives involving at least a couple of different companies and scenarios.

For example, the thirty-year-old father cannot be sure his daughter will even be alive when she is eighteen or nineteen years

Insurance for Combined Purposes

NN Financial: "Challenger"
Male, age 40, non-smoker
Female, age 40, non-smoker
Annual premium: $10,565   Interest rate: 7%
Contribution period: 20 years

Age	Annual deposit	Death benefit	Account value	Cash surrender value	Withdrawal
40	$10,565	$505,914	$5,914	$1,583	0
41	10,565	512,241	12,241	3,579	0
42	10,565	519,012	19,012	6,019	0
43	10,565	526,256	26,256	8,932	0
44	10,565	534,348	34,348	17,024	0
45	10,565	543,092	43,092	25,768	0
46	10,565	552,543	52,543	35,219	0
47	10,565	562,756	62,756	47,597	0
48	10,565	562,384	62,384	52,639	$11,384
49	10,565	560,914	60,914	54,417	11,725
50	10,565	558,797	58,797	58,797	12,077
51	10,565	556,170	56,170	56,170	12,439
52	10,565	565,824	65,824	65,824	0
53	10,565	576,153	76,153	76,153	0
54	10,565	588,514	88,514	88,514	0
55	10,565	601,938	101,938	101,938	0
56	10,565	616,517	116,517	116,517	0
57	10,565	632,351	132,351	132,351	0
58	10,565	649,547	149,547	149,547	0
59	10,565	668,223	168,223	168,223	0
60	0	678,517	178,517	178,517	0
61	0	701,839	201,839	201,839	0
62	0	734,876	234,876	234,876	10,000
63	0	740,581	240,581	240,581	10,300
64	0	746,467	246,467	246,467	10,609
65	0	752,542	252,542	252,542	10,927
66	0	758,812	258,812	258,812	11,255
67	0	765,283	265,283	265,283	11,592
68	0	771,964	271,964	271,964	11,940
69	0	778,861	278,861	278,861	12,298
70	0	785,983	285,983	285,983	12,667
71	0	793,338	293,338	293,338	13,047
72	0	800,934	300,934	300,934	13,439

TABLE VII

Insurance for Combined Purposes (continued)

Age	Annual deposit	Death benefit	Account value	Cash surrender value	Withdrawal
73	0	$808,780	$308,780	$308,780	$13,842
74	0	816,886	316,886	316,886	14,257
75	0	825,263	325,263	325,263	14,685
76	0	833,919	333,919	333,919	15,125
77	0	842,867	342,867	342,867	15,579
78	0	852,117	352,117	352,117	16,047
79	0	861,682	361,682	361,682	16,528
80	0	871,573	371,573	371,573	17,024
81	0	881,806	381,806	381,806	17,535
82	0	892,393	392,393	392,393	18,061
83	0	903,348	403,348	403,348	18,602
84	0	914,689	414,689	414,689	19,161
85	0	926,431	426,431	426,431	19,735
86	0	938,591	438,591	438,591	20,327
87	0	951,187	451.187	451,187	20,937
88	0	964,239	464,239	464,239	21,565
89	0	1,000,006	500,006	500,006	0

TABLE VII (continued)

old, let alone that she will go to university. Nor does he know for sure he will be able to manage a $2,500 annual contribution to the plan. The universal life plan provides a good deal more flexibility than a whole life plan, which allows you to deal with changing circumstances, but it will probably cost a little more in administration fees than simply investing in GICs. It requires more thought and management, particularly in making your investment decisions over the years. Look at investment life insurance if you believe it fits your needs. But don't get bamboozled by a soft shoe routine. To avoid the confusion of insurance costs, administration costs and yields, limit your choices to term-to-100 for the insurance element, and insist that the future cost of the life insurance be guaranteed. For comparison, use the same assumed premium with different companies, and choose on the basis of highest death benefit and/or most cash value at assumed death or retirement at age 70.

CHAPTER 7

Group Life Insurance

ALMOST HALF THE $1.3 TRIL-
lion in life insurance in force at the end of 1992 on the lives of
Canadians was group coverage. Most group insurance is offered to
people at work; sometimes it's an automatic benefit to all the employees at a company. Sometimes you're given a choice of taking
the policy or not, or of buying more than the minimum amount of
coverage. You can also buy group insurance through professional or
affiliation groups. A few of these groups guarantee life coverage to
new members, if you apply for the life insurance as soon as you join
the association.

The amount available in employee group insurance is usually defined by your salary. Common coverage is "one times salary" or
"three times salary." If your employer pays for your insurance, it's a
good deal. However, it's a misconception that group life is always
cheap because of the mass purchasing power of the group. In fact, it
is usually more expensive than individual coverage, especially for
younger individuals and non-smokers. In a group of 100 employees,
there will be a few with drinking or drug problems. Others will
have poor health histories involving diabetes, heart trouble, and
high blood pressure. Some will have dangerous hobbies such as car
racing, scuba diving or skydiving.

These are risks that the normal underwriting of individual policies identifies and weeds out. These people would be denied insurance at standard rates, and some would be denied life insurance
at any price. However, they would all be insured in a typical group
policy. Therefore, the expected mortality cost of the people covered
by a group policy will be somewhat higher than among those
covered with individual insurance. As a result, the premium might
be higher as well.

Most employer group policies require coverage of all eligible employees. If employees were allowed to choose, the insurance com-

pany would know that most of the poor risks would apply, but not all the healthy risks. In insurance, whenever customers are allowed to choose, it can only work to the detriment of the claims experience. This phenomenon is known as "anti-selection." The person who has suffered a heart attack or skydives on the weekend will rarely miss an opportunity to buy, increase or improve life insurance coverage. The healthy routinely pass up such opportunities. They'll even let life insurance lapse when in a financial bind, knowing it can be replaced.

The basic, mandatory coverage differs from individual insurance in that there is no suicide clause. Often there is the chance to purchase additional or "optional" group coverage. To buy the optional coverage you will probably have to take a medical or answer a questionnaire. Since there is a risk of attracting those contemplating suicide, this optional coverage contains a two-year suicide clause.

There are several disadvantages to group life. A group policy is owned and controlled by a sponsor, usually an employer or association. Therefore, you have no control over it. You will no longer be covered by insurance if you leave your employer although you may have the right to convert it to expensive permanent insurance. The insurance can be cancelled by the sponsor or the insurance company, or suspended during a strike. In hard times, companies may cancel their group benefits.

Association groups are notorious for failing to sustain a sufficient percentage of participation to make group benefits viable. (A notable exception is the group plan of the Ontario Medical Association, which is both stable and economical.) Because of these drawbacks, you should treat group benefits as a bonus on top of at least an adequate level of personally owned life insurance.

If you are offered the opportunity to buy additional group life coverage, compare the price with individual ten-year term insurance. Individual insurance could well come at a better price or provide better value in the long run. Let's look at some of the other advantages of individual insurance:

• the insurance is yours and will not cease if you leave your employer.

• you have complete control of the insurance. There is no risk that the policy will be cancelled or the insurance program renegotiated. Your current and future premiums will be published in the policy. (And, as a knowledgeable buyer of insurance, you will insist that they all be fully guaranteed.)

• you have the right to assign an individual policy to a bank as collateral. This cannot be done with most group policies. (Even if it could, would you want your employer to know all about your debts?)

• the entire individual policy is convertible to permanent insurance, such as term-to-100. Group coverage is usually convertible to permanent insurance, under certain conditions, particularly within thirty days of leaving the company, retiring or cancellation of the policy. But there may be a ceiling on how much can be converted, and conversion is usually limited to relatively expensive ordinary whole life policies, seldom a term-to-100.

With most group policies, you will be allowed to convert to a policy with a non-smoking rate only if you can prove you are in good health. This usually defeats the advantage of conversion since if you are not in good health, you might not be able to convert it. You'll find a competitive price by surveying the entire insurance market for any kind of permanent policy, including term-to-100.

Group coverage is of special significance to people with health problems that make them difficult to insure. If adequate insurance to protect your family is difficult for you to buy, look carefully at your prospective employer's group insurance when you consider changing employment. Convert your group coverage to an individual policy at each job change until you have built a portfolio of adequate individually owned policies.

CHAPTER 8

Choosing Your Options and Riders

OPTIONS ARE AS COMMON with life insurance policies as with cars. Some options allow you to make the policy fit your unique needs and, consequently, make it more useful. Others are frills that drive up the cost and serve little useful purpose. In this chapter, we offer our unabashed opinion of options.

Waiver of premium

The waiver of premium is the most commonly sold option on life policies. Under the option, the life insurance company will keep the coverage in force if you become disabled through sickness or injury but it will waive the premiums. Sometimes the cost of the option is built into the annual premium, but more often it's an extra cost.

It might seem to be a useful option: If you're ill or seriously injured, you would not want your life policy to lapse because the premium was not paid. In practice, the rider has little value. In most cases, the definition used in defining a disability in the waiver of premium is so restrictive that few people would ever qualify to collect. For example, in a Commercial Union Life Assurance Co. of Canada policy, the policyholder must be "not able to perform any of the duties of the life insured's usual occupation." If you can perform any of these duties, such as read a report, make a phone call, or dictate a letter, you would not be disabled in the eyes of the insurance company. The riders usually have exclusions, as well, that further limit the possibility of collecting any benefit. Typical exclusions are: "an accident which occurs while under the influence or affected by any drug or intoxicant, any self-inflicted injury, ingestion of any drug or poison."

Sometimes life insurance applicants are told the waiver of premium will even allow them to convert their inexpensive term insurance to a whole life policy, with cash values, while disabled and the increased cost of the policy will be covered under the waiver. In fact, although a few policies do allow such a conversion, in most cases once you invoke the waiver of premium you will no longer be able to convert from term to permanent. Your rights, or lack of them, will be reflected in the cost of the rider. The more expensive the rider, the more flexibility you'll have – maybe.

However, this rider is always costly for the coverage. Waiver of premium purchasers are not classified by occupation or health, the premiums are set at a high risk rate. Your life insurance premium is just one of many important obligations that would have to be satisfied if you were sick or injured. For this reason, you should insure your income with a good disability policy that would pay an adequate income regardless of how the disability occurred. (Disability insurance is covered in detail in chapters eighteen and nineteen.)

This is one of those rare situations where the best costs less. Typically, it would cost $97 to buy the waiver-of-premium rider for each $1,000 of life insurance premium. If you include your insurance premium as one of the living expenses covered by your individual disability insurance you would pay only $40 for each $1,000. Don't pay more than double the price for a disability protection riddled with exclusions.

Accidental death benefit

Double indemnity, also called accidental death benefit, can be added to almost any policy. This option doubles the death benefit if death is caused by an accident. Usually, death has to occur within ninety days of the accident. It is a poor choice. A family needs protection against your death; the cause of your death doesn't affect their need. They won't need twice the income if you die falling down the stairs rather than as a result of a heart attack. In fact, your family's need might be greater if you die from a long illness, especially if you are unable to work while ill.

Double indemnity can instill a false sense of security. Most of us can't imagine dying, and assume that if we do, it will be caused by an accident. In reality, fewer than 8 percent of deaths among people between twenty-five and sixty-five years of age are as a result of injuries suffered in an accident. Yet, like the waiver-of-premium rider, accidental death insurance is expensive.

If you have concerns about a particular family member who enjoys sports or dangerous hobbies, look into an accidental death and dismemberment policy. This could cover the whole family and provide an income or a lump-sum payment (or both) for broken bones, loss of sight and other major injuries. This type of policy does not cover illnesses.

Guaranteed insurability

Guaranteed insurability is a guarantee that you will be able to buy more life insurance in the future at standard rates despite any change in your health. The amount of extra insurance you can buy and the dates on which you can buy it are specified. For example, an option might offer an additional $500,000 of life insurance on the tenth anniversary of buying your policy. (Generally, you can expect to be sold life insurance coverage, including the future insurance of the guaranteed insurability option, that is about ten times your income. If you want more, you will have to submit financial data and justification.)

Guaranteed insurability often costs almost as much as simply buying the coverage outright. If you believe you will need the extra insurance in the future you might as well buy it now.

What might constitute a future need? Some business loans are conditional on life insurance being taken out to secure the loan. If you want a $1 million line of credit, the bank might demand $1 million of life insurance, or less coverage with a guarantee that you can get more in the future. If a business deal will require you to take over a substantial obligation, such as a mortgage, at a future date, then you might want to buy a guaranteed insurability option for that point in time.

Most companies will only issue guaranteed insurability options as riders on existing policies, they won't sell just an option. As well, they will usually not allow the value of future options to exceed the initial policy; that is, you cannot usually buy a $100,000 policy with an option to buy $500,000 more.

Insured loans

Often bank managers will offer you a life or disability insurance option on a loan. They are usually expensive and the coverage decreases as your outstanding loan decreases. It is possible you will need to borrow money but will be unable to buy a term policy to cover the loan because of poor health. If so, borrow from a bank where the loan insurance application fine print does not require you to make any declarations about your health. Bank employees who process insured loans may not be trained or licenced for life insurance. If you elect to use the bank's insurance option, read the forms carefully, and make sure the questions are answered accurately. Errors have resulted in death claims being denied.

Increasing the face amount

Some policies are sold with an option to increase the face amount of the policy by a set amount every year. Usually the death benefit will double over a specific period of time, such as ten years. The face amount of the policy can also rise to keep pace with the Consumer Price Index. Of course, the premium increases whenever the face amount increases. There are several advantages to this policy over buying another policy from time to time. First, the increase will come into force every year; if you decide to increase your coverage once in a while, death might strike just before an increase was planned but not yet in place. Second, the increases will be granted without any need for proving insurability. Most of us, sooner or later, have either a health problem or new sports activity that affects our insurability. Third, the increase takes place at a guaranteed premium. A locked-in premium schedule for future increases might very well be at much better rates than future rates. If the reverse occurs, the increase option can be declined, and separate insurance can be arranged. Fourth, since every policy premium includes an administrative annual fee of $50 to $100, regardless of the coverage bought, small policies tend to be uneconomical. By buying a policy that keeps pace with a growing need, you'll keep your annual fees low.

Insuring the cash value

There are also several policies on which you can insure the cash value. If you die, your family will receive both the death benefit and the cash value. If the policy makes sense in every other regard, this option is worth considering if you need increasing insurance. It's a popular policy in corporate insurance plans. The company can turn the policy over to the employee when he or she leaves at retirement, stipulating that the insured cash value be paid to the company at death. This split in the benefit allows the company to recover all, or most, of the premiums paid over the years. Universal life can provide this automatically.

CHAPTER 9

Evaluating Mail-Order Life Insurance

A FAVOURITE MAXIM AMONG life insurance executives is, "Life insurance is not bought, it's sold." The maxim explains the need to hire and train salespeople to reach customers who would not approach the company on their own.

But the maxim is not really true. Many Canadians understand the need to protect their families from the financial disaster caused by the premature death of a breadwinner. Many millions of dollars of life insurance are marketed through associations, credit card companies, and financial institutions as mortgage insurance.

These plans are often confused with group policies, but they are actually a hybrid, combining features of group and individual policies. They are usually more economical than group insurance, since they require medical evidence of good health, but can cost more than ordinary individual life insurance, since the medical requirements are less strict and the experienced mortality is higher.

The fact that a trusted association or company offers or endorses a mail-order plan does not make it a good buy. In fact, some of these plans are seriously flawed and should be avoided.

Let's assume you are in reasonable health and are willing to shop for your life insurance. You have carefully read this book, and believe you need $500,000 of life insurance, split between $300,000 of ten-year renewable term and $200,000 of term-to-100.

Many plans are available to you through the mail from charge card companies, university alumni groups, and professional associations. Few, if any, of the mail order groups can offer term-to-100 or ten-year term; they offer only five-year term. The limits on coverage, despite your health or occupation, are usually around $100,000 but sometimes a bit higher if you take a medical. Few of these plans allow conversion to term-to-100. Some don't allow conversion at all; they simply lapse.

Suppose you are a thirty-year-old non-smoking man. You could buy a $500,000 five-year renewable policy with Transamerica Life for $490 a year. This policy is convertible to Transamerica's competitively priced term-to-100 policy without a medical. The cost of this insurance is ninety-eight cents for each $1,000 of protection. The premiums for $1,000 of coverage through the Canadian Owners and Pilots Association recently are $1.92, and $1.04 as a member of the University of Western Ontario Alumni Association.

Such plans cost more than an ordinary, competitive term policy for several reasons. The application forms don't usually ask about occupational or vocational risks, therefore they might be of interest to people with dangerous occupations. (However, most brokers know which insurance companies will insure people with health problems or risky jobs at standard rates.)

Sometimes the insurance is expensive because the associations use the insurance plan as a fund-raiser. Sometimes the contract between an insurance company and the sponsor stipulates that after certain reserve criteria have been met the surplus premiums collected will be refunded to the sponsor. The sponsor can keep this money or pass it along to members of the group or association. (More than half of the premiums paid by the members of the Ontario Medical Association are refunded to the OMA. These are passed along to the members.)

Also, marketing life insurance through the mail is expensive. The companies spend thousands of dollars on brochures and postage to many thousands of people, a cost incurred without any guarantee of new business.

Consumers must be aware of other disadvantages to these policies. Most important, few carry as many guarantees as a policy purchased through an agent or broker. The insurance company or the sponsor often has the right to cancel the plan. (Individual policies cannot be cancelled by the life company as long as you pay the premium.) Most mail-order policies do not guarantee the future renewal rates. You will have to determine whether or not the policy is convertible to permanent insurance; and, if it is, to what you can convert. Few of the mail-order policies offer discounts for non-smokers, athletes or women.

If any part of the personal information you disclose might cause you to be turned down for insurance, you are much better off with an agent or a broker than with an application for a mail-order policy. In almost all the mail-order plans, once one of the questions is answered "yes" instead of "no" the application is rejected. An agent can discuss a health problem, suggesting further tests that might result in a policy. There is also the risk that, even if the policy is issued, it will not be valid at death if the insurer believes that you have not answered the questions on the application form correctly. One of the services of an agent or broker is the assurance that the application form is correctly completed.

If you live in a remote area, and do not have a local life agent or broker you can trust, shopping through the available mail-order plans might be an acceptable way to find coverage. It would still be preferable to find an agent or broker through the recommendation of a trusted friend or by telephoning the Life Underwriters Association or the Independent Life Insurance Brokers Association in Toronto for the names of several nearby salespeople. Making arrangements by telephone or by fax is an option.

CHAPTER 10

Term or Permanent?

SEVERAL FACTORS GO INTO
the selection of the correct policy for your unique needs, budget and
personality. The single most important consideration is the size of
the policy, because this will affect both cost and effectiveness.
There may very well be some excellent policies that you can't afford, so let's make life simpler by eliminating them right away. This
isn't any different than when you buy anything else: If you decide
to buy a new car, you might be convinced that the low depreciation
of a Mercedes-Benz makes it the most economical car on the road.
But, if you would not be comfortable with the cost of the car, you
won't seriously consider buying one.

Many insurance agents prefer to start every presentation with
some form of whole life policy. In the course of the presentation,
the premium comfort level of the prospective client becomes evi-
dent, and the face amount is adjusted to coincide with this comfort
level. This could mean reducing the death benefit that will be paid
to your family to so low a level that it will no longer provide the
protection they need. The policy size should not be tampered with.
If your budget is tight it is the bells and whistles that should be reduced, not the protection.

The "whole-life first" approach explains why there are hundreds
of thousands of consumers with $25,000 and $50,000 whole life
policies. These may be good, cost-efficient policies, with marvelous
flexibility and great cash values. The only problem is that they
won't do the job. A family that needs $400,000 to pay off the mort-
gage and fund an investment income for Mom and the kids is very
badly served by a $50,000 policy.

The second consideration is the time period over which you will
need insurance. If the need is short-term, for example, a bank
demand for life insurance to cover a two-year business bank loan,
the best policy is likely to be one-year or five-year renewable term.

If the need is permanent, perhaps to pay capital gains tax on a family business, then a whole life, term-to-100, or universal life policy is needed. But what kind of policy is best for the breadwinner who needs insurance for twenty or thirty years to protect his family?

Some insurance companies and their brokers and agents regard whole life insurance as the most flexible and effective insurance possible; others would argue for universal life. On the other hand, there are others who regard both as nothing short of a scam. The truth lies in between. In fact, the term versus whole life argument is the most hotly debated issue in life insurance marketing.

Let's take a closer look at some of the arguments you'll hear from the brokers and agents.

"Buy term and invest the difference."

This is common advice but will you be ahead if you buy a cheap term insurance policy instead of a more expensive whole life policy and invest the difference in cost?

To help you decide, we are going to look at three commonly sold policies and go through an analysis you might want to follow with the policies you're considering. We've used a forty-year-old man who doesn't smoke; he needs $400,000 in insurance. The whole life salesman might offer a policy that would cost $7,099 a year, pointing out that in twenty years the cash value would be $135,600. The client would pay $141,980 over the twenty years, putting him out of pocket only $6,380 for the insurance. "Just think," the salesman would say, "twenty years of insurance protection for only $6,380!" Of course, this assumes that the insurance will be dropped after twenty years – if it's not he won't get his $135,600 back.

The universal life broker would propose a plan into which the client would pay $2,426 a year for twenty years – $48,520. If he earned a 7 percent return on the funds he could withdraw $29,684 after twenty years and still keep the insurance paying a $2,426 premium every year. So, after twenty years the coverage would have cost $18,566 and he can opt to keep the plan in place.

The term insurance salesman might offer a ten-year term policy that would cost $606.50 a year for the first ten years and $1,970.50 a year for the second ten years. This insurance would cost $25,770 over the twenty years. The client gets nothing back after twenty years, but he can renew it for another ten years at an annual cost of

$5,746.50, or convert it to permanent insurance at an annual fixed cost of $9,254 for forty years.

In the first ten years, the term policy would be $6,492.50 cheaper each year than the whole life; $5,128.50 cheaper in the second ten years. If this money was invested and earned a 7 percent taxable return over the twenty years, the pool of investments would be worth $188,464. Obviously, he'd be well ahead, provided he had no further need of the life insurance protection.

This is a rather extreme example. The whole life policy we used, while quite popular, is one of the most expensive on the market. If we use a more conventional whole life product, perhaps one that costs around $2,374 a year, the insurance would cost only $47,480 over the twenty years and would build a cash value of $43,200. If our client bought the term insurance and invested the difference in premium, he would have about $38,772 in invested savings over the twenty years.

Now let's look at the universal life. The term insurance is $1,819.50 cheaper per year in the first ten years than the universal life policy; $455.50 cheaper in the second decade. If our client bought the term insurance and invested the difference in premiums he would have about $40,420 in savings, still assuming a return of 7 percent.

Buying term and investing the difference often is a better strategy, as far as it goes. But the "termite's" savings would rapidly deplete if he had to renew the term coverage at $5,746.50 for ten years and face a costly conversion to term-to-100 or whole life at a later date. If the game is over after twenty years, term is a better buy. But if it isn't, it isn't.

However, there is a flaw in the entire argument. The vast majority of Canadians who own whole life are dangerously underinsured. Most people need four or five times as much coverage as they now have through their whole life policies. If they own $100,000 in whole life but need (and switch to) $400,000 of term coverage, there would not be any significant money left to invest.

"Term insurance is temporary; whole life insurance is permanent. It will always be there to protect your family."
This is true, but it implies that either type of insurance can be sold in any situation. It isn't a valid comparison: Just as we don't compare cars with trucks when we're buying a vehicle, we shouldn't compare term insurance with whole life. Anyone with a short term

need for insurance would be poorly served with permanent insurance; and anyone with a permanent need is only postponing the inevitable with term.

Life insurance is usually bought to protect a flow of income. Many people do not need insurance in retirement since there may no longer be a risk of lost income to insure against. Adequate life insurance is needed during the years you are working; adequate retirement funds are needed in later years. The two demand very different financial planning. So why would we need permanent life insurance? Chances are, we won't. But what if life doesn't unfold as we expect?

A marriage late in life can create radically different needs. A man who marries a woman who is much younger than he might find himself unable to build an adequate estate to support her after he has died, especially if they have young children. He'll still be buying strollers and ballet lessons when other men are ploughing money into retirement funds. Even if they don't have children, she could outlive him by twenty years or more. A divorce can also cause a severe financial setback from which it will be difficult to recover in time to fund a normal retirement. And divorce agreements sometimes require a guaranteed payment to the estranged spouse, for life; the payment may even have to be life insured, as part of the divorce contract, so the death of the payer does not interrupt the payments.

Any one of your children could become disabled late in your life; this child could need care for many years after you've died. It would be very difficult for you to save enough to live comfortably in retirement and save enough to provide for that child's care.

On the other hand, you may become so successfully financially that you will need insurance to pay the capital gains tax or pass on a family business.

Look at your needs but keep in mind that even if our futures are uncertain we do not necessarily have to buy a permanent policy. Term insurance should always be purchased with a conversion option. This makes it just as permanent as whole life or term-to-100. If your needs change, you will be able to convert to the protection your family needs. Don't let the final conversion date pass without a final review of your needs.

"People who buy term won't invest the difference. They'll just spend it."

This is patronizing, and maybe it's true; but it's a poor reason to buy whole life. Your insurance policy should be purchased to fit your insurance needs: Only if you have a permanent need, should you buy a permanent policy; even then it should be the best buy you can find. Forcing yourself to save is outside the realm of this book; our only advice is that you should have the conviction to make your savings and investment plans work.

"Money spent on term insurance is money down the drain. With whole life insurance you're building cash values."

The cash value of whole life policies clouds the argument; remember, you receive the cash value only if the policy is cancelled. It's much like the resale value of a car; it's not a benefit unless the car is sold. If permanent insurance is needed to provide permanent protection, the cash values will never be received – the policy reserves will be used to fund the premium to death and the policy death benefit, as intended.

"The premiums on permanent policies always remain the same; the premiums on term insurance will rise every time you renew."

This is true. Of course, the term premium in the first years of the policy will be a fraction of the cost of the permanent policy. Your life insurance broker can use a computer that will compare the lifetime cost of two policies, assuming the difference in cost is invested. Make sure the policies chosen for comparison are both competitively priced. And don't compare apples to oranges; look at the policies that will fit your insurance needs. If you're buying term insurance, look at the term choices. If you're buying a permanent policy, look at the permanent choices.

"Whole life, term-to-100, and universal life insurance are very effective tax shelters."

This is true only of universal life, in which the policy reserve is kept separate from the death benefit. If the cost of the term insurance within the universal life policy is competitive – it often isn't – the tax sheltering of the savings of the policy can be very effective. It is then possible to pay for that insurance with tax-free investment income.

"Cash values in a life insurance policy are not only sheltered from taxes, but from creditors as well."
If you name a spouse or child as beneficiary of a policy, the money is considered to be held in trust for them, and cannot be claimed by creditors during the life of the policy owner or after his or her death. Such protection is lost if the beneficiary in the policy is listed as "estate."

Once you've established your need — both the amount of insurance and the time over which you will need protection — you will have to choose the policy. As we've mentioned before, the spread in rates among companies for similar life insurance policies is far greater than with virtually any other consumer product. Your next step is to decipher the price.

CHAPTER 11

Deciphering the Price of the Policies

THERE ISN'T A CONSUMER product on the market for which there are such vast differences in price for essentially the same thing. In mid-1994, one of the most expensive whole life insurance policies on the market would have cost $8,865 a year for $500,000 for a forty-year-old man who didn't smoke; the cheapest was $2,485. He would have found a similar astonishing difference in five-year term insurance. The most expensive policy would have cost $1,600 a year; the cheapest, $615.

Nobody wants to pay more than necessary for insurance but comparisons can be tricky. The adage, "You get what you pay for," is not necessarily true for life insurance. So how can you tell if you're truly getting value for your money? To figure it out, you must consider the three elements that affect the final cost of life insurance:

• annual premium
• dividends
• time

Life insurance is usually bought to be held for many years, and time is a critical factor in calculating its final cost. To be consistent with the usual practices in the insurance industry in Canada and the United States, all our comparisons will be over twenty years. In comparing policies, you must also keep in mind that money has an investment value; if you don't spend it, you can invest it. We will assume that any money saved is invested at 7 percent a year, or 4.2 percent after income tax.

The comparisons might seem daunting, but computer programs will survey all the policies of a particular type and rank them by cost. The programs can compare the different types of policies, and calculate which is the best buy.

It's also very important not to assume from an example of one type of insurance that one company is always the best choice, or another always the most expensive. Some companies can be very

Comparing the Cost of Term Policies

$500,000 insurance for a forty-year-old male non-smoker

Term of policy	Competitively priced policy		Expensive policy	
	Annual premium	Cost over 20 years	Annual premium	Cost over 20 years
1 year	$510	$86,105	$615	$87,880
5 years	720	33,650	1,600	55,525
10 years	740	29,600	1,255	36,900
20 years	1,060	21,200	2,615	52,300
Term-to-100	2,395	47,900	3,350	67,000

You can see that the annual cost of term insurance increases with the length of the term insured. The policies used to illustrate the competitively priced policy were not necessarily the cheapest available; however, the cost of the most expensive policies included in this table illustrate the tremendous difference in the cost of policies. It's vital for consumers to comparison shop when buying insurance.

SOURCE: COMPULIFE SOFTWARE INC.

TABLE VIII

competitive in some types of insurance but offer the most expensive policy for another. Different companies tend to "prefer" policyholders of a particular age, sex, or policies of a certain size.

Picking the cheapest term policies

Although a one-year term has the lowest initial premium, the cost of such a policy over five or ten years is higher than the longer-term policies. These policies are intended to be kept in force for only a year or two, usually for business purposes. The insurance company covers all of its costs of writing and selling the contract in that year, and repeats those costs every time the policy is renewed. Buying yearly renewable term is like taking a long trip by buying a series of short-hop tickets. It's possible, but expensive.

The most practical term for most people is the five- or ten-year term. The five-year is the most common, although the ten-year is usually slightly less expensive over time. Terms longer than ten years are generally not as practical as five- or ten-year renewable contracts. Although these contracts may be well-priced, the spreading of the cost of the insurance over the entire term means you will pay more in the early years. This isn't a problem if you can afford it, if you keep the policy until the end, and if your needs don't change.

A Present-Value Comparison of Five-Year and Twenty-Year Term Policies

Five-year term policies Issuing company	Cost*	Twenty-year term policies Issuing company	Cost*
Seaboard Life	$19,046	Transamerica Life	$16,418
NN Life	19,700	North American Life	16,626
Seaboard Life	20,009	North West Life	16,696
Equitable Life	20,125	Industrial-Alliance Life	16,696
London Life	20,387	Gerling Global Life	16,765
Transamerica Life	20,911	Laurier Life	16,898

*Over twenty years. Assumes a 7 percent present value.

SOURCE: COMPULIFE SOFTWARE INC.   SEPTEMBER 1995

TABLE IX

Should you change policies, though, you will have paid a higher premium in the early years without reaping the benefits of the lower cost in later years. The least practical term policy is term-to-age-sixty-five. Like other long-term insurance policies, it's expensive in the early years. More important, it's not good value. Some companies offer term-to-100 policies for less than what others charge for term-to-sixty-five.

Once you've decided which type of term policy to buy, ask your broker or agent to provide you with a survey of twenty or thirty firms and detailed quotes on the best six. Make sure the policies are convertible and renewable. A policy could have the cheapest premiums in the first term but uncompetitive premiums in the future. Always make sure these future premiums are guaranteed; if they're not, you could suffer an unpleasant surprise. The company could increase its rates to unacceptable levels.

Your broker can also calculate the cost of various policies over a variety of time periods. Such a comparison (called a present-value comparison) will tell you the total amount of money you will pay over the years you own the policy in terms of today's dollars. You can see in Table IX the difference in the present value of the premiums paid over twenty years for $500,000 of coverage bought by a forty-year-old, non-smoking man. The cheapest policy is Transamerica Life's twenty-year policy. Remember, though, this is term insurance which is not designed to meet a permanent need.

A Detailed Survey of Six Five-Year Term Policies

Male
Face amount: $500,000   Term: Five years
Age last birthday: 40   Age nearest birthday: 40   Non-smoker

Reliable Life Insurance Company
YRT-95(Star)-level premiums 1-5, 6-10

	Current	Guaranteed
Age 40		$615
Age 45		835
Age 50	$1,645*	4,135
Age 51	1,895*	4,650
Age 52	2,250*	5,270
Age 53	2,735*	5,975

Renewable to 95 Convertible to 50

Reliable Life Insurance Company
YRT-95(Gold)-level premiums 1-5, 6-10

	Current	Guaranteed
Age 40		$650
Age 45		900
Age 50	$1,795*	4,135
Age 51	2,035*	4,650
Age 52	2,375*	5,270
Age 53	2,835*	5,975

Renewable to 95 Convertible to 65

Seaboard Life Insurance Company
Select 5 - 5-year renewable

	Guaranteed
Age 40	$715
Age 45	1,090
Age 50	1,700
Age 55	2,595
Age 60	4,240
Age 65	6,905

Preferred rates apply to Super Select
Renewable to 75 Convertible to 70

Transamerica Life Insurance
5-year convertible & renewable

	Guaranteed
Age 40	$730
Age 45	1,275
Age 50	1,930
Age 55	2,755
Age 60	4,315
Age 65	7,885

Renewable to 80 Convertible to 71

Laurier Life Insurance Company
UltraTerm 5 - 5-year R & C term

	Guaranteed
Age 40	$739.50
Age 45	1,174.50
Age 50	2,024.50
Age 55	3,154.50
Age 60	5,254.50
Age 65	8,874.50

Renewable to 75 Convertible to 65

Seaboard Life Insurance Company
Select 5 - 5-year renewable term

	Guaranteed
Age 40	$750
Age 45	1,145
Age 50	1,785
Age 55	2,730
Age 60	4,460
Age 65	7,265

Renewable to 75   Convertible to 70

Legend: *value projected, not guaranteed
SOURCE: COMPULIFE SOFTWARE INC   AUGUST 1995

TABLE X

Summary of Other Companies Surveyed

These are the policies that were also surveyed to find the six most competitively priced policies in Table X. This survey is the second page of a typical computer survey. The policies are ranked by annual premium.

Male
Face amount: $500,000   Five-year term
Age last birthday: 40   Age nearest birthday: 40   Non-smoker

American International Assurance Life	$755
The Manufacturers Life Insurance Company	760
Gerling Global Life Insurance Company	760
Sun Life Assurance Company of Canada	765
Equitable Life Insurance Company	770
NN Life Insurance Company of Canada	785
Investors Syndicate	785
The Great-West Life Assurance Company	785
Mutual Life Assurance of Canada	790
London Life Insurance Company	793
Federated Life Insurance Company	795
The Standard Life Assurance Company	805
Financial Life Assurance Company	810
Royal Life Insurance Company Limited	860
The Canada Life Assurance Company	870
Co-operators Life Insurance Company.	870
Reliable Life Insurance Company Rg	880
Mutual of Omaha Insurance Company	920
The Canada Life Assurance Company	925
Wawanesa Life Insurance Company	935
Desjardins-Laurentian Life Assurance	935
The Imperial Life Assurance Company	935
Reliable Life Insurance Compay Rg	980
Union of Canada Life Insurance Company	1,155
Desjardins-Laurentian Life Assurance	1,600
Wawanesa Life Insurance Company	Below minimum age

SOURCE: COMPULIFE SOFTWARE INC.   AUGUST 1995

TABLE XI

Decreasing term insurance

Since the risk of death increases with age, the cost of term insurance usually increases over time. The exception is the decreasing term policy. The premium is level throughout the term but the face amount decreases. Decreasing term is seldom sold today, except as mortgage insurance by some institutions. Sometimes the in-

A Present-Value Survey of Five-Year Renewable and Convertible Term

This table compares the cost of six $500,000 term policies over time. They represent the least expensive policies in a survey of thirty-three policies ranked by cost over twenty years. The cost given for the policies is the total dollars spent at the end of each five-year period in today's dollars.

Male
Age last birthday: 40   Age nearest birthday: 40   Non-smoker

Seaboard Life Insurance Company
Select 5- 5-year renewable term

	Guaranteed
5 yrs.	$3,298.19
10 yrs.	7,391.34
15 yrs.	12,588.20
20 yrs.	19,046.09
25 yrs.	27,635.85
30 yrs.	39,023.66

Renewable to 75 Convertible to 70

London Life Insurance Company
5-year term non-participating R & C

	Guaranteed
5 yrs.	$3,660.30
10 yrs.	8,178.72
15 yrs.	13,737.83
20 yrs.	20,387.97
25 yrs.	28,934.68
30 yrs.	40,307.64

Renewable to 70 Convertible to 70

Seaboard Life Insurance Company
Select 5 - 5-yr. renewable term

	Guaranteed
5 yrs.	$3,459.64
10 yrs.	7,759.32
15 yrs.	13,216.02
20 yrs.	20,009.88
25 yrs.	29,045.33
30 yrs.	41,026.86

Renewable to 75 Convertible to 70

Canada Life Assurance Company
5-yr renewable term, non-convertible

	Guaranteed
5 yrs.	$4,013.18
10 yrs.	8,970.02
15 yrs.	14,961.69
20 yrs.	21,593.79
25 yrs.	28,512.19
30 yrs.	41,211.12

Renewable to 75

Equitable Life Insurance Company
5-year renewable and convertible

	Guaranteed
5 yrs.	$3,551.90
10 yrs.	7,814.02
15 yrs.	12,995.60
20 yrs.	20,125.42
25 yrs.	29,616.69
30 yrs.	42,431.07

Renewable to 75 Convertible to 65

Transamerica Life Insurance Co.
5-year convertible and renewable

	Guaranteed
5 yrs.	$3,367.38
10 yrs.	8,155.24
15 yrs.	14,055.20
20 yrs.	20,911.27
25 yrs.	29,652.97
30 yrs.	42,657.01

Renewable to 80 Convertible to 91

SOURCE: COMPULIFE SOFTWARE INC.   SEPTEMBER 1995

TABLE XII

Summary of Other Companies Surveyed

These are the other policies that were also surveyed to choose the six most competitively priced policies in Table XII. The cost reflects accumulated premiums for 20 years discounted at 4.20%.

Male   Face amount: $500,000
Age last birthday: 40   Age nearest birthday: 40   Non-smoker

Primerica Life Insurance Company	$17,044.16
The Maritime Life Assurance Company	17,113.73
Financial Life Assurance Company	18,087.68
The Great-West Life Assurance Company	18,087.68
NN Life Insurance Company of Canada	18,226.82
Norwich Union Life Insurance Society	18,644.22
Primerica Life Insurance Company Rg	19,479.04
Royal Life Insurance Company Limited	19,548.61
The Imperial Life Assurance Company	21,287.81
Desjardins-Laurentian Life Assurance	21,287.81
Reliable Life Insurance Company	21,357.38
Westbury Canadian Life Insurance Company	21,357.38
AXA Assurances	22,818.30
Toronto Mutual Life Insurance Company	23,653.12
Toronto Mutual Life Insurance Company	26,992.38
Mutual of Omaha Insurance Company	30,331.65
Westbury Canadian Life Insurance Company	36,175.36
Financial Life Assurance Company	Below minimum age
North American Life Assurance Company	Above maximum face
North American Life Assurance Company	Above maximum face

SOURCE: COMPULIFE SOFTWARE INC.   SEPTEMBER 1995

TABLE XIII

surance decreases by a set amount each year. Other policies are sold with coverage that remains the same for five years, then gradually decreases to nothing over twenty or more years. Such policies were sold to clients who, for instance, expected to need less and less insurance as their children grew up and their mortgages were paid off.

Since the insurance needs of families seldom decrease, this type of insurance is not usually needed. It's likely that inflation alone will decrease the value of any life policy fast enough, without having a built-in decrease. And, if your needs do drop, you can always decrease an existing policy. Almost all insurance contracts allow you to reduce your coverage at renewal. To clinch this argument, most companies charge no more for level-term policies than decreasing term. If you own a decreasing term policy, consider replacing it with a level term policy costing about the same.

Deciphering the cost of cash value policies

Comparing the lifetime cost of whole life insurance policies is usually clouded by the cash value. It shouldn't be. Whole life insurance should be bought to fill a permanent need for protection; for this reason, the cash value is of little consequence. Remember, the cash value is like a parachute that will soften the blow of a heavy loss of money if you must cancel your policy. Therefore, it should not be a major consideration in choosing a policy – and it is certainly not part of your cost comparisons. Don't add up all the premiums you'll pay over the year and subtract the cash value to arrive at a "net" cost. Such a calculation assumes you will cancel your policy.

Instead, to compare policies, add the premiums you will pay over the years until you reach age seventy-five. (This will be approximately the cost of the policy to death.) Once you've identified the cheapest policies, then look at the cash values of only those few policies.

If the insurance is bought to pay a capital gains tax on death or pass on a family business, cash values are of little interest. The policy will probably not be cancelled. If it is bought for ordinary family needs, situations do change. For example, if the insurance is on the life of a successful businessman to protect a wife who doesn't work outside the home, and she dies, the insurance would become redundant. In that situation, it would be nice to be able to cancel the insurance and receive a refund of the premiums.

When there is a possibility of needs changing, you might feel more comfortable with a modified term-to-100 policy that offers a refund of premiums – a cash value – after age sixty-five. If the policy is cancelled before age sixty-five, the insurance company keeps all the premiums and the policy reserves. After that age, there is a refund. These policies cost more than true term-to-100, but somewhat less than conventional whole life.

Term-to-100 policies

Because there are no cash values or dividends to cloud the cost of term-to-100 policies, it is easy to compare the cost of different term-to-100 policies – just add up the premiums paid over various periods of time. If you will be holding your policy for many years, it can also be interesting to compare term-to-100 to a ten-year renewable term policy, even if you don't have a permanent need. The term-to-100 will cost more than renewable term insurance initially, but the premium remains the same for the life of the policy. As a rule of thumb, the initial premium for term-to-100 is about the same, perhaps a little more, as the cost of a renewable term policy after ten years. If the insurance will be held well into old age, term-to-100 is much more economical than renewable term.

Consider the premiums and accumulated costs for a forty-year-old, non-smoking man who is not an athlete, using the most economical insurance of each type available in mid-1995. Renewable term, a ten-year policy, starts off at $740 a year, renewing in the tenth year at $2,680 a year. At the beginning of the twentieth year, it renews at $6,930 a year. For the first twenty to twenty-five years this is the most economical policy; however, if held past age sixty-five it becomes more expensive. In fact, in the thirtieth year, at age seventy, the policy would renew at an annual premium of $16,620. The term-to-100 policy has a level premium of $2,610 for the life of the policy and if held for thirty years the total cost will be $78,300. The ten-year renewable term would cost $103,500 if held for the same thirty years. Insurance buyers in their forties and fifties often have more disposable income and can pay more attention to economy, rather than price. While ten-year term is cheap in the early years of the policy, it may not be economical over the life of the policy.

Adjustable insurance

Life insurance differs from most financial arrangements in the very long periods of time over which it will last and in the array of risks being shouldered for you by someone else. In fact, although your insurance policy guarantees your beneficiaries will be paid a sum of money when you die, the life insurance company doesn't know when the money will be paid. It doesn't know whether an individual policy owner will die suddenly or even if the mortality rate in society will change. Until the early 1940s, infection often resulted in death. Today, infections are routinely treated by antibiotics. But now insurance companies face the costs that have risen along with the spread of AIDS. Finally, the company doesn't know what it will earn on its investments.

Comparing the Cost of Different Kinds of Policies

$500,000 insurance for a forty-year-old man

Policy type	Initial premium	Cost after 10 years	Cost after 20 years	Cost after 30 years
10-year term	$ 915	$ 9,150	$29,450	$75,450
Term-to-100	2,275	22,750	45,500	68,250
Whole life	2,345	23,450	46,900	70,350

SOURCE: COMPULIFE SOFTWARE INC.

TABLE XIV

Interest rates are a vital component in the calculation of the cost of a life insurance policy; the company assumes it will be able to collect and invest your premiums for many, many years before you die.

Insurance companies are in the business of accepting these risks but an adjustable policy softens the impact of fluctuating interest rates and mortality. The insurance company issues a policy based on current interest rates and mortality, but it reserves the right to "adjust" the cost, the benefits or both in the future to keep the policy in line with reality.

Some, unfortunately only a few, companies spell out exactly what mortality and interest rates assumptions they have made, and the impact which any changes will have. Most simply advise that they will set a new premium and/or death benefit every five or ten years.

You can assume that a 2 percent change in interest rates will usually cause your premiums to shift inversely by 10 percent. That is, if interest rates drop by 2 percent, your premiums will rise by 10 percent. If interest rates rise by 2 percent, your premiums will fall by 10 percent. This gives the company tremendous flexibility and it can give you the advantage of lower premiums if interest rates climb or mortality falls. But it could also work against you. If you are offered an adjustable policy, use this checklist to make sure you understand what you're buying:

• Is there a ceiling on the premium you might have to pay?
• Is there any limit to how much the coverage can be reduced?

• Is there an alternative to an increase in premium, such as the replacement of some of the whole life insurance with term insurance or a longer premium-paying period?

• Is the interest rate used to adjust the policy tied to an outside indicator such as a GIC rate or is the policy adjusted at the company's discretion?

• Are the non-forfeiture values (the cash and paid-up values) guaranteed or are they also adjustable?

Whatever you do, don't buy a policy in which the mortality charges can be adjusted. The interest-rate risk is difficult enough.

Understanding the costs of universal life policies

Analyzing the cost of a universal life policy is simpler if you distinguish the savings and the insurance and compare the two separately. First, look at the cost of the insurance as you would in any other policy. You'll find many universal life policies cannot stand up to the scrutiny; the insurance is usually expensive. The company will offer high guaranteed future premiums and indicate it intends to charge less if you remain in good health – something which you cannot guarantee. A few companies do not offer any guarantee on future premiums at all. Eliminate these policies from your analysis. Never buy insurance without guaranteed future premiums.

The returns on the savings are either a choice of investment funds or a guaranteed interest rate. Some companies offer a range of prevailing interest rates at daily, annual, one-year, five-year, ten-year, or longer terms. Comparisons are difficult since a company could have very attractive interest rates on savings but very high insurance premiums, too.

In every universal policy you will be able to set your own premium level but there will be a minimum and maximum range you will have to remain within. Call one company for the minimum and maximum premiums that it would accept and, for the purpose of comparing policies only, set a premium midway between the two. Ask your broker to get quotes from five companies – only those that guarantee their premiums – based on paying that annual premium to age sixty-five. (If your salesperson is an agent tied to one company, you should request these quotes from his competitors yourself.) Ask for two quotes: one with a stable death benefit, a second with a death benefit that increases with the cash value. Ask them to assume the current interest rate to age sixty-five. (The companies will automatically deduct the insurance costs and fees.) Be sure that the same interest rate assumption is used on all quotes.

From these quotes you can rank them two ways, by cash value and by death benefit. The company with the highest cash value will be the one that deducts the least from the savings account for the life premiums and administrative expenses and credits the highest interest to the savings accounts. It will not necessarily have the highest death benefit. Your best policy will be one of the top two or three on either list. You should then choose the company that offers the best guarantees on future insurance costs.

If you want to invest in a mutual fund type of investment, ask your agent or broker to compile similar quotes but only from those companies that offer equity investment options.

To make sure you understand the policies being offered to you, ask all of these questions:
- Are the premiums on the life insurance guaranteed?
- Are the premiums level or increasing?
- What would the annual insurance deduction be if all the invested funds were withdrawn at age 65?
- How much are the plan administration fees?
- Are they guaranteed not to increase?
- How many investment choices are available?
- How well have the equity funds performed in the past? You could even look at the performance of the company's funds by studying the monthly mutual fund tables in *The Globe and Mail* or in *Understanding Mutual Funds*, a companion book in the Personal Finance Library published by Globe Information Services.

Choosing your premium paying period
The actual costs of paying for a policy for ten, fifteen or twenty years or over a lifetime are the same since the costs are founded on the same financial considerations – the cost of paying death benefits, meeting office expenses and the interest that can be earned on any money in reserve. In practice, one or the other scheme will have more appeal, since it will be a better match to your personality. If you take pride in paying off debts, loans and mortgages as quickly as possible, paying off a life insurance policy promptly will have definite appeal.

If, in fact, you'd like to pay for your insurance as quickly as financially possible, you could find it complicated comparing the policies you'll be offered by various companies. Suppose you are forty-six years old and would like to buy a $500,000 policy. Company ABC offers a non-par policy guaranteeing that eight annual payments of $8,408 will pay off the premiums while Company XYZ offers a policy with an annual premium of $6,115 that will be paid in eleven years. A few calculations will show that these offers are about equal; that is, eleven times $6,115 equals eight times $7,815, if you give credit for interest earned on the difference.

When the costs of the two offers are similar, you have to look at other factors, such as cash values and guarantees. In this case, the only guarantee in Company XYZ's policy is the $6,115 premium. The company forecasts that, given current interest rates, mortality, costs and taxes, you will not have to pay a premium after eleven years; but this isn't guaranteed. If, in fact, taxes increase, interest rates fall, and mortality increases, you would have to keep paying past the eleventh year, perhaps much longer.

The guaranteed policy is guaranteed only because the insurer takes a conservative view of the future; the premiums will be a bit higher and the cash value a bit lower. In our example, the forecast cash value difference between the two policies at age seventy-five is substantial – in the policy offered by Company ABC the cash value will be $142,000, but in Company XYZ's policy it will be $237,000. However, the guaranteed cash values in the two policies are similar – $142,000 for XYZ and $129,000 for ABC. (Company ABC guarantees the $129,000, it only forecasts that dividends will bring the cash value up to $142,000.)

If there is a chance at some future date that life insurance will not be needed, you should buy the participating policy with its more generous cash value. If it was certain that the policy would always be needed, the cash value is of no interest and the peace of mind of a guaranteed premium is more important.

Par versus non-par policies

Every agent, when proposing a participating policy, will illustrate the proposal with the future dividends assumed to be similar to the dividends currently being paid. The proposal will state clearly: These dividends are not guaranteed nor are they estimates of dividends to be paid in the future. Actual dividends will vary with company experience, and may increase or decrease each year.

Insurance companies in Canada try to portray probable future dividends, but the 1982 federal budget contained a good example of the risk inherent with a participating policy. It introduced the tax on investment income of life insurers. This was a flat tax on the gross investment income of the insurance companies.

It had not been anticipated, and became a cost that affected the cost of new policies and had to be absorbed by existing policies. Policyholders with guaranteed premium policies were not affected. Those with adjustable and participating policies faced the consequences: higher premiums or lower dividends.

One company had sold policies in which future dividends were to be used to pay off the policy by the end of the eleventh year. The effect of the new tax was to postpone this to between seventeen and twenty years. The policy might have been a good idea at the time it was bought but was not if premiums had to be paid at least six extra years.

Fortunately, this experience is far from typical. Actuaries' assumptions about future interest rates, costs and mortality tend to be based on current experience for the first few years, and then become gradually more conservative for the later years. As a result, unless interest rates and costs do adversely change, the dividends tend to rise dramatically with time. In fact, they can become larger than the premium. When this happens, policy reserves exceed the requirements to pay the cost of the insurance.

There are five common options for dividends in a participating policy.

1. They can be taken in cash each year.

2. They can be used to reduce the annual premium. This option tends to steadily reduce the net premium due each year until there is no premium due at all, and the policy owner is advised that he or she can stop paying premiums. In theory, adverse experience at a later time could reduce future dividends and you could be expected to start paying premiums again. This is unlikely but possible.

3. They can be left on deposit with the insurance company in one of several types of investment accounts. While the dividend itself is not taxable (since it is a refund of part of your premium), returns in the investment account are subject to the usual tax rules. Equity funds are a popular choice for investing dividends.

4. They can be used to buy "paid-up additions" – small paid-up policies, each with its own cash value and dividends. You will not have to pay any other premiums to keep these policies in force. Nor is there any medical or other underwriting information required

providing the option is elected when the policy is originally issued. Paid-up additions are much more expensive than the normal cost for insurance at the same age.

5. Dividends can buy a decreasing term policy designed to decrease at the same rate the paid-up values increase. In this way, the initial face amount of the term policy is "enhanced" by the future value of the paid-up insurance. For example, if the paid-up value at age sixty-five is to be an additional $100,000, the policy would be issued with a $100,000 "enhancement" – the decreasing term part of the policy. As the paid-up value increases, the term policy decreases. The policy owner enjoys the higher level of protection from the first day, but the "enhancements" are not usually guaranteed after the first five years or so.

Participating policies may be more attractive in theory than in practice. Companies dislike giving back large sums of money as generous dividends. They create "special" funds as "security" for the policies. When the policies are cancelled or terminated at death, the money in the special reserves is not paid out. It remains in the company, the property of the remaining participating policyholders.

One of the most basic and commonly sold life policies in Canada is five-year renewable and convertible term. In 1992, 25 percent of these policies were par policies; 75 percent were non-par. If you look at the survey on page 72 of the six cheapest five-year term rates for a $500,000 policy on a non-smoking forty-year-old man, you'll find they all offer competitive rates in the first five years. However, there is a wide disparity of guaranteed renewal rates.

On the policy we looked at in chapter four, the guaranteed maximum renewal rate at age fifty-five on the participating policy offered by Mutual Life is almost double that of the other company – $5,760 rather than $2,805 on the policy from Transamerica Life. The company expects that the dividends would reduce the cost to rates similar to, or even better than, the guaranteed premiums. If you bought this policy, it would tie you to very high future premiums and the hope that dividends would reduce your cost. Is it worth the risk? As you can see from the survey, the forecast "net cost" is no better than the guaranteed rates available. You would be accepting risk in return for eventual costs that will be similar to guaranteed premiums.

Your purchase

Once you know how much you need and the kinds of policies you would like to buy, it's a simple matter to ask your agent or broker for a computer survey of various different kinds of policies – perhaps ten-year renewable term, twenty-year renewable term and term-to-100. This survey should show the cost and features of twenty or more companies. From this you should be able to choose the most economical policy. Remember, economical means not only that the policy is well priced compared to other policies but that it also suits your income, both now and in the future.

We know it can be hard to be sure you are paying a fair amount for your insurance. We hope the tables on the following pages will guide you not only in buying insurance but in evaluating the insurance you already own. The premium comparisons are based on $400,000 of life insurance and were compiled in July 1994 using information which Compulife Software Inc. maintains on some forty-five life insurance companies.

As you can see, prices vary widely between the lowest and highest premiums for a particular product. You'll also notice that one company is not consistently the least expensive. In some cases, the highest premiums in one situation were from companies with the lowest premiums in another.

It is also important to keep in mind that the actual results of the survey depend on the amount of insurance you're buying, your date of birth and your health. The rates used in the surveys were for individuals of "regular" health risk. Some life insurance companies offer discounts for "preferred" life risks and their premiums could be marginally lower than those shown.

The surveys of five-, ten-, and twenty-year term do not consider the lifetime cost of these policies. Most renewable term policies provide a renewal premium guarantee. These renewal premiums can vary even more dramatically from company to company. Sometimes, the company with the lowest initial costs can have extremely high renewal costs. It might be in your best interest to select a slightly higher-priced policy to obtain a better renewal guarantee.

If you're choosing a whole life policy, you will have to decide whether it's necessary to measure both the cost of the death benefit and the cost of the cash value. In either case, you'll need fresh batteries for your calculator to figure it out.

A Buyer's Guide to Ten-Year Term ($400,000)

Age	Sex	Smoker	Lowest company in survey	Lowest premium	Highest company in survey	Highest premium
25	M	No	Sun Life	$415	Financial	$780
	F	No	Westbury	272	Colonia	672
	M	Yes	Sun Life	567	Reliable	1,140
	F	Yes	Gerling	360	Reliable	1,140
30	M	No	Sun Life	371	Financial	688
	F	No	Westbury	272	Colonia	672
	M	Yes	Sun Life	611	Reliable	1,140
	F	Yes	Westbury	432	Reliable	1,140
35	M	No	Laurier	474	AEtna	754
	F	No	Empire	358	Colonia	680
	M	Yes	Gerling	860	Blue Cross	1,292
	F	Yes	Westbury	584	Reliable	1,140
40	M	No	Laurier	606	Blue Cross	1,008
	F	No	Empire	498	Blue Cross	840
	M	Yes	Metropolitan	1,246	AEtna	1,850
	F	Yes	Maritime	898	Blue Cross	1,492
45	M	No	Laurier	906	Blue Cross	1,424
	F	No	Westbury	640	Primerica	1,150
	M	Yes	Financial	1,824	Blue Cross	2,668
	F	Yes	Westbury	1,212	Blue Cross	2,112
50	M	No	Financial	1,340	Union of Canada	2,072
	F	No	Financial	880	Primerica	1,690
	M	Yes	Financial	2,788	AEtna	3,970
	F	Yes	Financial	1,700	Blue Cross	3,096
55	M	No	Financial	2,208	Blue Cross	3,380
	F	No	Financial	1,340	Primerica	2,726
	M	Yes	Financial	4,220	AEtna	6,054
	F	Yes	Financial	2,400	Primerica	4,658
60	M	No	Financial	3,336	Assumption Mutual	5,968
	F	No	Financial	2,112	Blue Cross	3,976
	M	Yes	Financial	6,056	Assumption Mutual	8,888
	F	Yes	Financial	3,224	Blue Cross	7,008

SOURCE: COMPULIFE SOFTWARE INC.   AUGUST 1995

TABLE XV

A Buyer's Guide to Five-Year Term ($400,000)

Age	Sex	Smoker	Lowest company in survey	Lowest premium	Highest company in survey	Highest premium
25	M	No	Sun Life	$403	Desjardins	$728
	F	No	Transamerica	314	Union of Canada	740
	M	Yes	Sun Life	567	Reliable	1,140
	F	Yes	Laurier	441	Reliable	1,140
35	M	No	Sun Life	419	Desjardins	920
	F	No	Financial	336	Desjardins	800
	M	Yes	Laurier	761	Desjardins	1,388
	F	Yes	Laurier	601	Reliable	1,140
45	M	No	American	875	Desjardins	1,800
	F	No	Financial	604	Desjardins	1,548
	M	Yes	Gerling	1,652	Desjardins	2,708
	F	Yes	Gerling	1,060	Desjardins	2,068
55	M	No	Financial	1,996	Desjardins	3,480
	F	No	Financial	1,196	Desjardins	2,980
	M	Yes	Union of Canada	3,644	Desjardins	7,484
	F	Yes	Financial	2,152	Desjardins	5,688

TABLE XVI

A Buyer's Guide to Twenty-Year Term ($400,000)

Age	Sex	Smoker	Lowest company in survey	Lowest premium	Highest company in survey	Highest premium
25	M	No	Royal	$488	Westbury	$1,104
	F	No	Financial	364	Westbury	1,076
	M	Yes	North American	738	Westbury	1,564
	F	Yes	Financial	564	Westbury	1,448
35	M	No	Laurier	690	Westbury	1,484
	F	No	Laurier	530	Westbury	1,244
	M	Yes	North American	1,132	Westbury	2,656
	F	Yes	North American	842	Westbury	2,152
45	M	No	Gerling	1,428	Westbury	3,116
	F	No	Maritime	994	Westbury	2,432
	M	Yes	North American	2,734	Westbury	5,696
	F	Yes	North American	1,726	Westbury	4,528
55	M	No	Financial	3,320	Westbury	7,728
	F	No	Financial	2,100	Westbury	5,820
	M	Yes	North American	6,094	Westbury	11,340
	F	Yes	North American	3,354	Westbury	9,184

TABLE XVII

A Buyer's Guide to Term-to-100 ($400,000)

Age	Sex	Smoker	Lowest company in survey	Lowest premium	Highest company in survey	Highest premium
25	M	No	Union of Canada..$952		Desjardins...............	$1,326
	F	No	Metropolitan..........698		Union of Canada.......	1,268
	M	Yes	AXA 1,402		Industrial Alliance	2,032
	F	Yes	Western 987		Union of Canada.......	1,720
35	M	No	Royal...................1,528		Union of Canada.......	2,044
	F	No	Royal...................1,212		North West	1,724
	M	Yes	Laurier........... 2,439.50		Westbury	3,384
	F	Yes	Royal...................1,828		Union of Canada.......	2,508
45	M	No	Equitable.............2,915		Union of Canada.......	4,468
	F	No	Laurier.................2,215		Maritime	3,510
	M	Yes	Seaboard.............4,753		Industrial Alliance	6,392
	F	Yes	Seaboard.............3,369		Maritime	5,862
55	M	No	Laurier........... 5,835.50		Union of Canada.......	8,764
	F	No	Laurier........... 4,247.50		Union of Canada.......	6,648
	M	Yes	Transamerica.......9,146		North West	13,084
	F	Yes	Transamerica.......5,902		Union of Canada.......	9,052

Lifetime coverage with premiums level for life. Policies have no cash-surrender values or reduced paid-up values. Lifetime coverage with premiums level for life. Policies have no cash surrender values or reduced paid-up values.

TABLE XVIII

Whether buying term, term-to-100 or whole life, you have to shop carefully. Insist that your agent provide you with quotations from a number of life insurance companies and don't hesitate to obtain a second opinion. Many agents have access to the Compulife survey reports used in this book.

CHAPTER 12

Choosing a Broker or Agent

TRADITIONALLY, BUYERS OF life and disability insurance have not been very knowledgeable. Income insurance is complicated and, frankly, dull. There is little incentive − as there is with a sporty new car − to shop around and explore the market before buying.

Few people approach an insurance agent or broker knowing exactly what they want. At best, they know they need insurance and they rely on the salesperson's advice, but they resent being pushed. That's why life and health insurance is usually sold rather than bought. It also explains why insurance companies have developed elaborate marketing organizations over the years to distribute their products. Two distribution methods we've already discussed are group insurance in chapter seven and direct mail in chapter nine; but without a doubt, the most powerful selling force in the industry is the brokers and agents. It's important to understand the difference between the two.

Only about a dozen of the 155 or so life insurance companies in Canada maintain networks of branch offices staffed with agents licenced by provincial authorities to sell life and disability insurance to the public. These companies recruit and train their agents to market their products. A career agent sells primarily his or her own company's products, and has the considerable advantage of the company's resources.

Life insurance is a complex product that is difficult to sell. Branch managers operate a continuous recruiting and training program. Prospective agents are tested for aptitude in selling, and a major requirement is usually a list of at least one hundred sales prospects whom the new agent could approach. After basic training, the agent is expected to arrange selling interviews with his prospects, including family, friends, past co-workers, and acquaintances. Many agents fail to graduate from selling to this group to selling to the general public. Those who do undergo continuing education with their own companies and/or a professional association.

Most companies, including many of those with career agents, also sign contracts with independent sales representatives, called brokers, so that their insurance is available through brokerage offices as well. The typical broker is an ex-agent who has given up the support and security of working for a major insurance company to have the flexibility and independence to offer the products of a variety of companies. He or she must still be licenced provincially. Although the typical broker has contracts with up to a dozen or more companies, he actually sells the products of only a few. He's restricted by the difficulty in keeping track of the numerous policies offered by even a handful of insurers.

Many life insurance brokers in Canada subscribe to a computer survey service operated by Compulife Software Ltd. of Kitchener, Ontario. This service allows them to call up current insurance rates on their personal computers. Using computerized rate manuals, a broker can make sure that he or she offers competitive rates. You shouldn't assume that a broker will automatically survey rates from a number of companies or that an agent won't. Brokers, however, are generally less restricted in their ability to shop around, and are more likely to have an idea of the range in prices for a particular type of insurance.

Brokers must take other considerations into account apart from premiums, including the quality of service (to the broker as well as to the client), commissions, underwriting service, and completeness of a company's product line. Although in theory all companies are financially sound, the broker must also recognize that some are in better shape than others, and may choose to ignore some suspect companies. Sovereign Life, Les Cooperants and Confederation Life are recent examples of companies whose operations have ceased because of unsolved financial problems.

Most life insurance companies have an excellent network of support personnel to back up their agents and brokers, including legal and accounting experts to help with the complexities of estate planning and business insurance.

How insurance people are paid

Some people involved in the complex distribution system for life insurance are on salary, such as secretaries, marketing support personnel, and commission clerks. Others are on combinations of salary and commission, such as branch and unit managers, field superintendents, marketing directors, and vice-presidents of marketing. The salespeople – the agents and brokers – are on straight commission.

The income for all these people, and more, comes from your premiums. Although a salesperson may have arranged to draw against commissions to smooth out some of the peaks and valleys in income, agents and brokers are paid solely on production. Their commission contracts set out the commission, bonus and renewal commission for each type of insurance product. Whether you deal with an agent or a broker, the commission arrangements are similar.

Commissions vary from contract to contract and from company to company. However, the variation tends to be in how the commissions are split over the first three years rather than differences in total remuneration. For example, one company might pay a commission equal to 100 percent of the first year's premium in the first year and 25 percent in the second. Another company might pay 75 percent in the first year and 50 percent in the second. A third might pay 75 percent in the first year, 25 percent in the second and 25 percent in the third. The agent's or broker's commission also depends on his or her experience. A new agent in the business receives a relatively low commission, say 50 percent of the first year's premium in the first year and 15 percent in the second.

However the broker or agent is paid, the total commission paid by the company for the sale of a policy might very well be 200 percent of the first year's premium and 100 percent of the second year's premium. The extra commission goes to the supervision staff above the agent all the way up to the company's vice-president of marketing.

As the agent develops more expertise and requires less supervision, his or her share of commission increases through a bonus system. Although there are differences among companies, one universal feature is that commission rates are higher for big producers. Commission tables are usually presented as a "basic commission" for each product, usually between 50 and 75 percent of the premium. Another table sets out a bonus based on volume. An agent producing over $100,000 in new annual premiums could expect a bonus of about 50 percent. Bonuses are expressed as a percentage of commission, not of premium. Thus, a 50-percent commission could be raised to 75 percent if the agent qualifies for a 50-percent bonus. The first-year commission, with bonus, runs between 75 and 125 percent of the premium.

New agents are expected to take time to build their commissions to a reasonable income. Until the new agent does so, he or she is allowed to draw against future commissions. After becoming a regular producer, the salesperson is expected to pay off the debt, and just take commissions as earned. By the second year, the agent is receiving a substantial renewal commission, as each of his first-year policies renews. This provides a basic income that can be counted on.

If you pay your premiums monthly, your agent may only receive a commission based on the monthly premium. Some companies are more generous with their agents, and "annualize" the commission. For example, if you paid your premium monthly with a $100 cheque, the agent's commission might immediately reflect the $1,200 annual premium. If you put a stop payment on your preauthorized cheques in the first year, the agent would be debited for most of the commission already received.

Some companies require an agent to represent them for a number of years before the renewal income "vests." That means that if the agent leaves the company, but stays in the business, the renewal commission will continue to be paid. This policy serves as a golden handcuff to keep the agent with the company. Other companies offer contracts stating that the renewal commission will be paid to the agent as long as the agent has a licence.

Almost all companies require life insurance to stay in force for two or three years before the high commissions paid in the first two years are considered "earned." If you buy a policy but don't renew it the second year, there is a good chance the agent will have to pay back all the bonus on the sale and at least half the commission. If you cancel a policy, count on the agent calling on you, since he or she has a strong interest in your maintaining the policy.

An agent who sells a policy to a client is expected to service that client forever. Service includes administrative duties such as processing changes in beneficiaries, processing bank assignment requests, and keeping track of changes of address. In return, the agent receives what is called a servicing renewal commission. After the client pays each year's premium, the agent also receives a renewal commission of 2 to 10 percent.

If the agent has been in business for a number of years, the volume of work generated by routine service is significant, but so is the renewal income. An experienced agent could expect to have renewal income of $5,000 to $10,000 a month.

As you can see, your agent or broker is well paid. Do not be shy about asking for service.

Conflict of interest

Any commissioned salesperson faces a conflict of interest when advising customers to buy. After all, the more you buy, the more he or she makes. Similarly, the surgeon will not earn a surgical fee by advising against surgery; the lawyer will make less by advising against a lawsuit.

The commissioned insurance salesperson faces a second conflict; sometimes the commission paid on one insurance product is far more lucrative than on another. For a broker, the conflict can be even more acute since different life insurance companies pay different commissions for similar policies.

Some companies make a deliberate attempt to sway their agents by offering poor commissions on renewable term policies and high commissions on whole life insurance. Canada Life, for example, pays the broker 30 percent of the premium on the sale of a five-year term policy but 75 percent on term-to-100. If a client needs $300,000 of insurance, the agent could offer the term policy with its premium of $366 (on which he would earn $110) or term-to-100 with its $917 premium (on which his commission would be $687). Put another way, the commission for $100,000 of whole life is $400 but the commission for $300,000 of five-year term is $110, yet the premiums are very close. Which product do you think the insurance company wants sold?

Brokers face the same conflict when comparing policies from various companies. A computer survey of quotes for a client might reveal that the policies from Gerling Global and Financial Life are both competitive – but Financial Life pays 50 percent more commission. He would probably recommend the Financial Life policy, a decision he would justify by the fact that his continued survival in the business is also important to his client. This might be acceptable if the two premiums were similar but the same decision when the two premiums are quite different would be more difficult to defend.

Choosing your broker or agent

In buying life and disability insurance, there is no advantage in choosing an agent over a broker, or a broker over an agent. What matters is that the person be an experienced professional who will fulfill your needs now and in the future. All agents and brokers are licenced either directly or indirectly by their provinces or territories. Only Quebec recognizes the legal existence of the broker. There, a broker is defined as an insurance intermediary who "offers life insurance to the public on behalf of two or more insurers, and is not bound by exclusive contract to any of them." This is as good a definition of a broker as any, and many thousands of agents in other jurisdictions would also qualify as brokers under it.

Brokers might be sponsored by one company, but they have contracts with several others, typically at least four or five. Each contract arranges to pay the agent or broker for business placed with that company, and none of the contracts requires that the agent or broker sell that company's products exclusively. In Newfoundland, agents who place business with other companies must seek written permission from the sponsoring company each and every time a policy is sold with another company.

A professional, conscientious agent representing one company can serve your needs, as can a professional, conscientious broker who owns an insurance business. The former probably knows how to bring the wide range of support services of his company to bear, whereas the independent has the backing of support systems from organizations catering to the independent agent industry.

Your representative must be experienced in the area of insurance you require. Group insurance, pension planning, corporate insurance, and family insurance are all distinct specialties. The person must be interested in handling and administering your type of insurance policy. The agent who handles the group insurance of major corporations is unlikely to be experienced with $250,000 family term policies.

If you don't have an agent or broker, ask friends and co-workers to recommend one. In fact, you should find two people who appear to be interested in your business, making sure one is an independent broker. They should have been in the business for at least five years so that you have some assurance that they will remain. Ask each to prepare a proposal for your life insurance needs, and then question both carefully. Choose the person who combines the best of price, service and empathy.

What makes a good agent or broker

As the insurance consumer, you should ask questions, understand the issues, and compare the proposals from the people who want to sell you insurance. As long as you do so, none of the ways of marketing insurance offers a clear-cut advantage over the others.

But that is not to say that it doesn't matter who sells you insurance – far from it. We suggest you look for these qualities:

1. You want someone who will be available without fail to serve your future needs. Do not consider someone you know who has recently gone into the business. Friends, acquaintances and especially relatives are not appropriate. We say this not just because of the uncertainty about whether the person will be in business five or fifteen years down the road. Your life insurance will be a long-term, ongoing proposition, and even if the agent stays in the business, it is awkward to have an arm's-length, professional relationship with a family member or long-time friend. How do you discuss such personal matters as marriage breakup, income tax problems, and secret health problems with your brother-in-law, or your ex-brother-in-law?

Insurance company training and the continuing education programs from professional associations are very good, but it takes time and experience to be really effective. An agent who has stayed in the business for five years has sufficient experience to serve your needs adequately and will probably be in it for a lifetime. If the agent has only been in the business for a year or two, this is much less likely.

2. You may be most comfortable with an agent your own age, or one who is no more than ten years older than you. Again, since this will be a long relationship, you want someone of your generation, or close to it. People close to you in age will communicate better and be able to understand your approach to life better than someone your parents' or children's ages.

3. A good agent will be willing to take the time to discuss your situation, plans and aspirations. As a reader of this book, you will ask more thoughtful questions than the agent is used to hearing, and a good agent will take the time to give you thoughtful answers. He or she may even say, "I don't know, but I'll find out." That is usually a sign of a secure, professional attitude.

4. A good agent won't necessarily agree with your assessment of your insurance needs. In this case, he will state his position and, if you are not persuaded, will carry out your wishes.

5. A good agent will respect your needs on price. You can't afford to waste money on life insurance. There are many companies offering each type of life insurance. You should make it clear that one of your needs is reasonable price and good quality. This means that any company/policy quoted should rank, say, in the best ten for price. An agent who won't comply may have agreed to an exclusive contracting arrangement that puts his security ahead of your needs.

In most cases, agents representing only one company will be able to find a competitive product within their company's range of products that meets your criteria of policy type and price competitiveness.

Failing this, the agent should be able to assure you that his company will give permission to place your business with another insurance company. Otherwise, look for another agent.

Your responsibilities as a consumer

No matter how much faith you place in your agent, you must take responsibility yourself when you buy insurance, and the first responsibility is to pay the premium. It doesn't matter if the invoice gets lost, you change your address, or the post office loses your cheque. Obviously, the insurance company and the agent/broker will try to advise you when a premium is due, but thirty days after the due date, the policy may lapse if the premium is not paid. In such circumstances, the company is under no obligation to reinstate the policy or honour a claim.

If you pay annually, make note of the due date. Better yet, authorize the company to take the premium out of your account when it is due, whether you pay monthly, quarterly, semi-annually, or annually. Preauthorized cheques are the most reliable way to pay premiums.

For your own security, make your cheque payable to the insurance company, not the agency or the agent. Mark your policy number on the cheque, so there is no doubt as to which policy it is paying for.

Whenever seeking important information, whether before or after an insurance purchase, ask for the answer in writing. In most instances, this will assure you that the answer has been vetted by a responsible source. Even if an error is made, a letter on company or agency letterhead should be sufficient to assure ultimate satisfaction.

Whether you deal with an agent or a broker, your intermediary should carry errors and omissions insurance, also called malpractice insurance. This is for your protection, and any conscientious agent wants to be sure that you would not suffer through his or her error. In such situations you need more than apologies. You need an agent with sufficient financial backing to make full restitution. Some provinces do not require agents to protect the public in such situations so make sure you require it.

CHAPTER 13

Life Insurance in Business

SO FAR, WE HAVE DISCUSSED life insurance only as a way of creating a cash benefit at death that will be used by the deceased's family. In the large majority of cases, that's the reason for buying it. But a cash payment at the insured's death can also come in very handy in business.

Buy-sell agreements

Buy-sell agreements are legal documents that help business owners ensure a smooth transition of ownership and control at death. This is important if the beneficiary of the deceased shareholder's interest is his or her spouse, particularly if it's unreasonable or undesirable for that person to have an active role in the business. A buy-sell agreement also ensures that there is a market for the shares – a problem with privately held companies.

Of course, a buy-sell agreement requires funding, and the most common source is life insurance. Although the insurance is a business expense, the premiums are not deductible. However, the death benefit is tax-free.

There can be several ways to structure a buy-sell agreement. These are the most common:

1. The corporate stock redemption method: The company owns the policy, pays the premium, and is the beneficiary. If the shareholder dies, the company buys the deceased's shares from the family with the insurance proceeds. The family does not receive a capital gain but a deemed dividend instead; this means there is a tax cost.

One of the advantages of the corporate stock redemption method is that there is less risk that the party responsible for the premium neglects to pay it, causing the policy to lapse.

2. The promissory note/deferred sale method: This is often preferred. The company again owns the policy, pays the premium, and is the beneficiary. When one of the shareholders dies, the surviving shareholders buy the deceased's shares from the estate using a promissory note. The company receives the insurance and puts the money into its capital dividend account. From there it is paid out tax-free to the surviving shareholders, who in turn use the proceeds to pay off the promissory note.

The deceased's estate will be subject to capital gains tax, unless the shares pass to the spouse at cost. In the latter case, the spouse will be responsible for the capital gain.

3. The hybrid method: A mix of the two previous methods. The company is the owner and beneficiary of the policy, and pays the premiums. In this case, the buy-sell agreement is structured to take effect under the promissory note method to the extent that a capital gains exemption may be available. For any capital gains beyond the deceased's unused capital gains exemption, the company buys back the remaining shares.

4. The split-dollar method: The company and its shareholders share ownership of the insurance policy, and premiums are paid by both (but the bulk by the company). When a shareholder dies, both the company and the surviving shareholders receive death benefits. The company's benefit roughly reimburses it for the premiums it has paid; the surviving shareholders use their proceeds to buy the shares from the estate or the surviving spouse. The tax result to the deceased's estate is generally the same as with the promissory note method.

5. The criss-cross method: The simplest because no corporate ownership is involved. Instead, each shareholder is insured by a policy owned by the others. The surviving shareholders simply buy the deceased shareholder's shares with the insurance proceeds. The tax result to the deceased's estate is generally the same as that under the promissory note method.

The criss-cross method protects the insurance proceeds from corporate creditors. It also removes a risk that, by increasing the company's inactive asset levels, the insurance proceeds could make the company's shares ineligible for the $500,000 capital gains exemption available to qualifying small businesses. In addition, this method reduces the fair market value of the shares.

Insurance used for any of these buy-sell agreements is usually permanent insurance, rather than term. However, based on personal preference and individual circumstances, it could be either, except under the split-dollar method. In this case, the insurance must be permanent because the policy must build up a cash surrender value. This allows the company to recover the premiums it has paid if the insured shareholder sells his shares and leaves the company.

All of this is complex. Unlike some other life insurance purchases, insurance for buy-sell agreements is not something you should buy without professional help. Not only do you need the services of an insurance agent or broker specializing in buy-sell insurance, but those of a lawyer and an accountant as well.

Key person insurance

There is a second use for insurance in business. Some business ventures are dependent on one person. A multimillion-dollar investment on the worldwide tour of a popular singing star would be lost if the star died and you didn't have insurance on his or her life. Many companies also have a star who is vital to the operation's survival. In such situations the company buys insurance on the life of this key person, naming the company the beneficiary. This makes the shareholders, partners, and even the bank, more secure.

Every type of insurance requires an "insurable interest" – the policy owner must stand to lose something before insurance can be arranged. With key person life insurance, the proposed owner, the company, must demonstrate need for the insurance and show a potential loss at least equal to the insurance.

The person being insured must sign the life insurance application and all medical forms. If you are being insured in such an arrangement, insist that the life policy be cancelled or sold to you, should you leave the company.

Living benefits

We mentioned earlier that "life insurance" is not a very accurate label. It's really death insurance because, traditionally, it has paid benefits only at death. At the end of the 1980s, however, life insurance suddenly changed. In limited circumstances, life policies sold by Canadian companies are now paying "living benefits" while the policyholder is still alive.

There are two quite distinct types of living benefits, one of them especially useful for small business owners and professionals. This type of living benefits policy combines some features of life and disability insurance. An ordinary disability policy pays a monthly income, or in rare cases a lump sum, for all causes of disability except those specifically excluded in the contract (such as intentional self-inflicted injuries or acts of war).

The living benefits policy, on the other hand, pays at death and in the case of specific occurrences. "Occurrences" is the operative word because neither disability nor death need take place.

For example, a policy may provide a payment if the insured person develops cancer. But many people have a tumour removed without suffering a disability, or at least one not lasting more than a short time. The same is true of heart-bypass surgery and an organ transplant. Of course, some occurrences that trigger insurance payments are disabling, such as blindness and paraplegia.

Other occurrences that can trigger payments, depending on the policy and the insurance company, are kidney failure, stroke and dementia. The occurrence may trigger the payment of the full face value of the policy (although there may be a maximum), 50 percent, or 25 percent, according to the policy wording. The rest is paid at death.

Depending on the policy and the insurer, the living benefits policy may be issued as a specific contract, but limited to certain dollar maximums, or as a rider to conventional life policies.

Obviously, it would be advantageous to have as many different "triggers" as possible listed in the policy.

Why would you need a large lump sum if you suffer a major health setback but expect to be back at work in months? There are several reasons. First, coping with a debilitating disease or terminal illness will dramatically change your life — and your cost of living. You might not be able to work, or you might be told to cut back on the hours you work to be able to recover. At the same time, there will be heavy medical expenses. Living benefits policies are designed to help pay for rehabilitation; or, where a terminal illness has been diagnosed, lump-sum living benefits could be used to "make a dream come true."

Another major reason might be income tax. Business owners and professionals often alter their year-ends, usually to January 31, to defer taxes. However, an altered year-end means you are perpetually behind in your taxes, paying last year's taxes with this year's income. If your cardiologist urges you to take it easy while you recuperate from bypass surgery, that may be difficult to do if at the same time Revenue Canada is hounding you for tax payments. A life insurance policy paying a living benefit provides a tax-free lump sum that can be used to pay your back taxes, permanently removing the burden of tax arrears.

Business partners and professionals can also use living benefits to generate funds if one partner ceases to be able to work effectively. Insurance proceeds can be used to buy a disabled partner's shares.

The other type of living benefit is a Canadian-originated concept that has spread to the United States. In the most common Canadian version, it is not a contractual obligation but rather a voluntary advance payment that can be made if the life-insured becomes terminally ill.

If a policyholder with AIDS, terminal cancer or heart disease, Lou Gehrig's disease or other life-shortening conditions asks, the company might provide some of the death benefit while the person is still alive. In effect, this is a loan against the soon-to-be-paid death benefit. The lump sum can then be used to do something the dying person could not otherwise afford, such as providing specialized medical and nursing care.

A precondition is that the beneficiary must give up rights to the insurance proceeds. The amount payable depends on several factors, but a key factor is the time the person is expected to live. The shorter the life expectancy, the larger the amount the company will be willing to pay.

Paying out living benefits of this type does not cost the company anything, since the proceeds are repaid, with interest, from the death benefit when the policyholder dies. If you're in this situation or know someone who is, there's nothing to lose by asking the company if they will consider offering the benefit. If you're buying coverage, you should consider a good living benefits rider as a contractual provision of the policy. But remember, such advances may upset the original purpose of the insurance – family protection.

Taxation and life insurance

Under the Income Tax Act, the expense of buying life insurance is not deductible. However, loan expenses can be deductible if the loan is for income-producing purposes. Revenue Canada's Interpretation Bulletin 309R has been used for many years by insurance agents, accountants and tax planners as a guide to how life insurance premiums can be deductible if they are a required expense of a loan.

In such circumstances, the taxpayer usually has a letter from the bank, offering to provide a loan only if it can be secured by life insurance. This situation arises typically when someone is setting up a non-capital-intensive business that depends solely on the skills of the business owner, such as in a consulting business. The bank may be confident in this person's ability to pay off the loan, but death would stop the income and leave no significant business assets.

Revenue Canada takes the view that the only deductible insurance (when part of a loan) is the simplest term insurance. Even the slight additional cost of a conversion option would not be considered part of the deductible premium.

Since virtually all premiums would include such a "frill," it has been the practice to buy a suitable new policy or pledge an existing policy to the bank, and claim only that part of the premium that would be equal to a bare-bones term policy.

In 1991, a technical amendment to the act (20(1)(e.2) was passed setting out new rules defining how life insurance can be part of a deductible loan expense. This brings the act into line with actual practice. It also defines how policies other than pure term insurance can be used as collateral. The ability to use term-to-100 insurance as deductible collateral is most interesting.

Under the act, the income tax department recognizes the deductibility of an annual term policy with a premium that escalates every year. This premium would soon surpass the cost of a level premium policy, such as term-to-100. At that point, the taxpayer who pledged a term-to-100 policy to the bank would be able to deduct 100 percent of the cost of the term-to-100 policy. When the bank no longer requires the insurance as collateral, the taxpayer will own a policy that has been heavily subsidized through deductibility. In the case of a policy that has been entirely paid for, there obviously won't be any more premiums to pay.

If the policy is owned by the taxpayer's company, it could then be sold to the insured for $1 and, as long as it had no cash value at the time of transfer, there would be no deemed benefit for tax purposes. Some policies have very high cash values that become available only after twenty years or at age sixty-five. If the transfer took place before this cash value date, the taxpayer would have received the corporate money tax-free.

CHAPTER 14

Insuring the "Uninsurable"

"UNDERWRITING" IS A TERM that goes back hundreds of years to Britain where the first insurers were individuals who were willing to assume someone else's risk of economic loss in return for a price, or premium. The person putting up the money usually wrote a contract, the insurance policy, and signed at the bottom to indicate he was accepting the risk – he was "underwriting" the risk.

In those days, underwriting insurance contracts was strictly a speculative business because it lacked an essential ingredient of modern insurance: comprehensive statistics that allow insurance companies to predict accurately how much they will have to pay out in death benefits in a given year. In modern parlance, insurance company underwriters are the people who assess the risks that underlie the setting of premiums.

Life insurance companies have standards that define risk, so that the appropriate premium can be charged. The four major characteristics considered are:

• Age. Younger people pay less than older ones.

• Sex. Because women have a longer life expectancy than men, they can expect to pay about 10 percent less for insurance than men of the same age. (However, women are far more likely to suffer a disabling illness or accident and pay as much as 40 percent more than men for disability insurance.)

• Smoking habits. Non-smokers pay about half as much as smokers.

• Health. This includes your current health, your past health history, and even your genetic family history.

The more insurance you apply for, the greater care an insurance company will take in analyzing the risk. Similarly, the older you get, the more thorough the examination and testing. Around 95 percent of people who apply for life insurance will be found to be "standard" risks. This does not mean perfect. A standard risk might be a bit overweight, have slightly elevated blood pressure, or even be mildly diabetic. However, these items are cumulative, and if enough little things are less than ideal, a person can be considered a "substandard" risk.

If the applicant is in better-than-average health – a marathon runner, for instance – this person may be able to pass a medical and qualify as a "super select" risk.

If you are overweight or are being treated for high blood pressure, don't be deterred from applying for life insurance. Every application is considered on its own merits. In fact, some companies make a point of trying to insure people at standard rates who have been turned down elsewhere.

If your health is not good, or the insurance company takes a dim view of your history of flying, scuba diving or skydiving, ask your agent to send the underwriting information to several other companies. Even if a number of companies say you are a substandard risk, and would therefore demand a higher premium, it may not be the last word. You can ask for a policy at standard rates with an exclusion stating that the policy would not pay for death caused by skydiving – or flying or dirt-bike racing. Take this step only if you no longer indulge in the dangerous activity.

Some applicants are found to be substandard after surgery, or after such problems as dizzy spells that may indicate underlying health problems. The insurance company may offer to issue the policy with an additional premium, called a "medical extra" or a "rating," but promise to review the rating within five years and remove it if the condition has improved. This is a fair offer. In the meantime, you could try other companies every year, in hopes of receiving a standard offer.

Finally, if the rating is offered on a permanent basis because the health problem is permanent, such as a very poor family history or a heart condition, ask the agent to compare the premium quoted to the premium paid by older people for the same policy.

A premium of 30 percent more may sound excessive, but if it means paying the same premium as someone just five years older than you, it may not seem so bad. After all, the insurance company is saying that your life expectancy is about five years less than average. This might strike you as a reasonable assessment. Before accepting any rating offer, make sure your agent has tried several companies, and find out the age at which someone of standard risk would pay the premium being offered to you.

If the premium translates to the premium of someone much older than you, perhaps the company is overreacting; or perhaps you do not realize the gravity of your health problem. Even if you are declined insurance at standard or even substandard rates, your agent will be able to find you "guaranteed issue" policies that have no underwriting questions other than your age and sex. They're expensive, but if you have a serious problem and need the insurance, they are worth the extra money. A typical guaranteed issue policy would pay a benefit of only the premiums paid if death occurs in the first year. But it would pay a third of the face value in the second year, two-thirds in the third year, and the full death benefit in succeeding years.

If you have been warned that death is imminent, but this is neither publicly known, nor obvious, see if there are any associations that you can join that guarantee some group life insurance to new members. Some groups guarantee that the first $25,000 or so is available with no questions asked.

And now we come to AIDS, or acquired immune deficiency syndrome, which has become a factor in underwriting. It has been more than a decade since AIDS entered our collective consciousness on a wave of fear.

The killer virus caused particular concern among life and health insurance companies because, if insured people die prematurely from AIDS, it follows that they will collect their insurance earlier than the actuarial assumption. This represents a triple loss to the insurance company: the death benefit, the interest lost because of the early payment, and the loss of years of future premium payments.

In Ottawa, the Superintendent of Financial Institutions, concerned with the possible effect of AIDS on the solvency of life insurers, asked companies to reconsider the adequacy of their reserves. The companies did so, and many announced they were setting aside extra reserves to allow for claims caused by AIDS.

In 1987, one insurance industry report suggested that AIDS would cause Canadian life companies to pay $2.3 billion in extra benefits during the following twelve years. And as late as 1988, the chief executive officer of a major life company told policyholders that AIDS "will require all insurers to increase premium rates."

However, except for a handful of isolated premium increases attributed to AIDS – and one of them had to be rolled back when sales declined – the worst forecasts have not come to pass and it now appears that they won't.

Not only have AIDS deaths not increased as dramatically as some predicted, but the extra claims have been offset by greater investment earnings by insurance companies, a gradual increase in life-expectancy and a decline in smoking.

In addition, life insurance companies now require applicants to undergo blood tests for even small life insurance policies. People with AIDS or the related HIV are refused insurance. Ironically, there has been an added financial benefit for life insurers. As part of the increased screening, blood samples are subjected to more tests. As a result, unreported use of high blood pressure medications, as well as the use of cocaine and other illicit drugs, are being detected. So the more stringent underwriting procedures are reducing claims from other causes.

On the other hand, it was estimated a few years ago that from 5 to 19 percent of the people who tested positive for AIDS antibodies would eventually contract the disease and die. Recent experience suggests that the figure may be close to 100 percent. Another factor working to push up premiums has been a new federal tax on life insurance companies.

So at any given time, some factors tend to increase insurance premiums and others tend to reduce them. Competition and such moderating influences as longer life spans and less smoking suggest that the long-term trend of lower premiums may continue, if at a slower pace due to prevailing low interest rates.

CHAPTER 15

The Application Form

THE WORD TO REMEMBER IS "application." Unlike other things you might buy, insurance takes more than money. You have to qualify. Insurance companies are very careful about the people they insure, and the greater the risk the more care they take. The application form is a vital part of obtaining insurance, and forms a legal part of the final contract.

The life insurance company is interested not only in your current health but also in your medical history. Many insurance applicants are nervous about the health history part of the application because they can't recall exactly when they had their appendix out or were treated for an ulcer. Don't worry. An estimated date is acceptable. Vagueness about the nature of the medical problem is not. If your application reads "Surgery 1977" with no explanation, questions will be asked. You will save yourself time by being more explicit with something like, "Late teens, hernia surgically repaired. No complications or reoccurrence."

Don't withhold relevant information. If you neglect to mention that you race cars, fly airplanes, or skydive, you are taking a chance in more ways than one. If you were to die in a skydiving accident, and had not mentioned this activity, the claim would probably be contested. If the insurer could prove that it would not have issued the policy at standard rates knowing that you were a skydiver, a court would probably rule that the company does not have to pay the death benefit. This applies even if your death is caused by something else. If you died in a traffic accident and the company found out about your skydiving, it could contest the policy.

The questions are straightforward, and usually easy to answer. For those active in work- or sport-related activities that might be risky, you'll be given a special questionnaire to provide the necessary information. Many activities, such as flying an aircraft or scuba diving, are usually insurable at ordinary rates. But if you state on the questionnaire that you enjoy test-flying homemade aircraft or exploring underwater caves, the application will probably be turned down.

Your answers on a life insurance application today do not limit your activities in the future. If you take up an uninsurable activity later, the policy would remain valid unless the company could prove to a court that you took out the policy knowing you were about to embark on a risky activity.

Honest mistakes are not held against you. Your insurance can't be cancelled or benefits denied because you forgot details. In fact, to deny a claim the insurance company has to prove fraud, which would involve a deliberate withholding or distortion of information. Insurers are not so sympathetic to smokers who think their smoking habit is unimportant: If you fail to disclose your smoking on an insurance application, you risk making your policies invalid. Courts have confirmed that insurance companies are within their rights to refuse to pay death claims to smokers insured at non-smokers' rates. To help prevent honest error in the ticking off of the various boxes on the application, some companies require the applicant to declare their smoking status in writing. Someone who writes, "I have not smoked or used any form of tobacco during the last year," is making an unequivocal statement.

The application will also cover your hobbies, sports and occupation, as well as your family's health history. Most insurance companies then have an independent investigation company check into the accuracy of the information provided. A week or so after you apply for insurance, you can expect a phone call from an investigator who will ask you to answer many of the questions you have already answered on the application. Any discrepancy in the two sets of answers you have given will be given close attention.

Depending on your age and the size of the policy you are applying for, some additional medical information will be required. If you have seen a physician during the last five years, he or she will probably be asked for a summary of your health history. (You authorize the doctor on the application to release this information.)

Except for the smallest of policies, increasingly thorough medical examinations are required. While an application for a $25,000 policy may only require you to answer "yes" or "no" to questions, anyone wanting a $5 million policy will have to submit to examinations by two specialists well known to the insurance company, complete with a chest X-ray, an exercise electrocardiogram, and urine and blood tests. You can be sure that the latter two tests include screening for alcohol, drugs, tobacco, AIDS and other potential risks.

You can also expect to be asked about your income. While you may think this is none of the company's business, it is important that there be a reasonable relationship between an applicant's income and the amount of life insurance being applied for. After all, in the most common life insurance situation, the insurance is intended to replace the applicant's income. Applicants for more than $500,000 in insurance will often be asked to complete a detailed questionnaire on their assets and liabilities. The company is likely to question an applicant who wants more than about ten times annual income.

The application sets out the name and relationship of the insured, the policy owner, and the beneficiary to be sure the three have what insurance companies call "an insurable interest." A wife could buy a policy on her husband and name her children as beneficiaries, but she would not be allowed to insure a friend with whom she had no financial relationship.

Once completed, a brief summary of your application is filed with the Medical Information Bureau. This lists your name and date of birth, plus a code for any underwriting conditions of interest. For example, there is a code for various health conditions, such as heart ailments or diabetes, and for occupations, such as that of pilot.

The bureau is not allowed to supply specific information to an insurance company, but might tell it that a previous insurer noted something of interest. The bureau does not receive copies of medical or test results. The purpose of the bureau is to keep applicants from failing to report such health-related matters as heart attacks. This helps keep Canadian life insurance about the cheapest in the world.

CHAPTER 16

Backing Out of an Insurance Purchase

EVERY NEW INSURANCE POLICY must be "placed," in the industry vernacular; that is, it must be delivered to the client and all outstanding requirements must be satisfied, including payment of the first premium, fulfilling medical obligations, and obtaining the client's signature on any amendments and policy receipts.

Once all of these requirements have been met, the policy is considered placed. The agent can then expect to be paid, and the clock is ticking on a ten-day "free look" by the policyholder. Within this period – ten days after the client has received the policy, as set by law in most provinces and territories – he or she can mail it back to the agent, branch office, or head office, and expect a full refund of the premium.

For this reason, you should immediately read a new policy to make sure that the wording conforms with the agent's explanation. Some policies are complex, and occasionally, an agent may give an incorrect explanation. Remember that the policy is the contract, not what the agent has told you. Pay special attention to your copy of the application and the results of your medical examination that should be included with the policy. The danger with your application form is that the agent may have recorded your name, age, occupation, income or hobbies incorrectly. If these pages are not included, return the policy and ask that they be included, specifying that you will not accept the policy until you have had ten days to review all relevant documents. This would start the ten-day free look over again.

Since you have signed the application, the company will hold you accountable, and any misrepresentation (deliberate or not) can later bring the validity of the policy into dispute.

During the "free look," the insurance company is on the hook to pay a full death benefit. But it will refund the premium, without any requirement for explanation, if cancellation is requested within the ten days.

Agents and companies don't like to see cancellations. They have gone to considerable effort and expense to underwrite the application and get the policy issued, so cancellation will cost them money.

But suppose you discover a terrible flaw in your new policy, or find a better policy at a much lower premium, several months after issue, and want to back out. First, if you have been paying a monthly premium, your loss if the company won't make any refund will be much less than if you have paid the full annual premium in advance. If you are trying to cancel some type of renewable term policy, your best bet is to arrange for your new policy, making sure it is in force, and then stop payment on the monthly payments of the old policy. If the old policy was an annual premium plan, you can use the period while the new policy is being underwritten to write to the old company and request a change from annual to monthly payments, and a refund of the balance of the premium. They might comply with this request.

If you really want to stretch your value for the premium dollar, ask the new company to make the new policy effective on the thirtieth day after the last premium payment on the old policy. You are fully insured during this grace period, so you will enjoy a month of insurance for free.

If the old policy was a permanent type, you will have a significant loss of value if you cancel the policy, since the mortality cost to the insurance company over the first year will be much less than the premium paid. However, if you have found a better value policy within the first year, it will likely be in your best interest over the long run to make the change, even if you have to lose all the premium paid.

It is worth the effort, however, to recover some of this premium. Negotiate with the company and see what you can obtain. The company has insured you, and has been on the hook. It would be fair if the company kept enough of your premiums to pay for a full year's annual renewable term insurance of the same face value as the permanent policy.

You should appreciate that the agent and the company will be unhappy, and probably uncooperative. Be honest with yourself, and decide who is to blame. If you have arranged insurance without shopping around first, you are to blame, and should be prepared to chalk up all or part of the loss to experience. In this situation, ask the agent, in writing, with a copy to the company, that the permanent policy be changed to term, with the full premium paid credited to the term policy. After the credit has been used up, you can replace this policy with the one you should have bought in the first place.

If the agent has been negligent in failing to properly explain the policy, or failing to properly explain the options open to you, tell him what you would like done. Say you blame him for the problem and will give him the opportunity to set the situation right. Explain that if he will not, or cannot, satisfy you, then you will have to complain to the insurance company and/or the provincial regulator.

If you have to go above his head, have the problem well documented. If the agent has failed to properly explain or disclose the facts, you should have your notes from the presentation (if you took them) and, better yet, his presentation papers. If you are right, can prove it, and are polite yet firm and persistent, you have about a fifty-fifty chance of a refund. As a sign of good faith and understanding, your request for a refund should include the offer to pay the insurance company a full year's premium for a yearly renewable term policy, so the company can be paid for its underwriting costs and time on risk.

If the policy is more than a year old, you can't expect any refund unless you can clearly prove blatant misrepresentation on the part of the insurance company or the agent. In such cases, it might be better to approach the insurance company first, to give it the opportunity to sort the problem out, before you involve the provincial regulator.

Make it clear that the company has a specific, limited period to arrange satisfaction before you will be obliged to go to the regulator. This is not a threat, but a courtesy. If the company is unaware that the agent has been doing something wrong, it will want to investigate, and put a stop to it. Give the company a fair chance. If it lets you down, take the problem to the regulator. Federal and provincial regulators are listed in the appendix.

CHAPTER 17

Replacing an Existing Policy

FOR BOTH THE AGENT OR broker and the client, the decision to replace an existing policy is a difficult one. You should act cautiously.

We're not arguing that you should never replace a policy. Sometimes it can make sense to you as a consumer, even though the industry is united in its condemnation of the replacement of policies. Switching hurts everyone, the industry argues, with companies losing as much as they gain. Life companies want quality business, business that stays on the books. Lapses and cancellations are expensive for the companies. The cost of the advertising, underwriting, commissions, and policy issuance are all borne in the first year. It takes years before the policy becomes profitable. If a policy lapses or is cancelled during the first five years or so, the company will probably lose money.

Older policies are even more profitable for insurance companies. The cost of life insurance has fallen dramatically over the past twenty years. Premiums are now half to a third of what they were in 1970 because interest earnings on reserves have been much higher than had been expected. Yet mortality is somewhat less. Finally, existing policyholders are an important source of new business to an insurance company. If the client leaves, the company loses contact, and will probably lose all future business with that client. So life companies are very protective of existing clients. Replacing a policy will also hurt the agent or broker who sold you the policy; both his or her commissions and bonus would be cut.

But is replacing a policy good for you? When you buy a new policy you are going to have to pay all those commissions and fees and administrative costs again. Those costs will be reflected in a higher premium, delayed dividends, or a slower buildup of cash values. You'll also be subject to a new two-year suicide clause and incontestability period. This could result in your family not receiving a death benefit if you died within two years because of suicide or an inaccuracy on your application, even if the inaccuracy was unintentional. Every insurance company has the right to cancel a policy within two years if it believes the application to have been false; after the two years are up, the only way an insurance company can cancel a policy or decline to pay a death benefit is if it can prove there was fraud in the original application.

These arguments are all valid. But they also ignore the vast difference in the price of insurance policies. Therefore, before you decide to switch, or not, you have to compare the cost of keeping your old policy with the cost of buying a new one.

Unfortunately, calculating the cost of an old policy is even more difficult than calculating the cost of a new one. The life insurance business is an unusually unfettered industry. Unlike the securities industry, life insurance companies do not have to disclose future premiums, deductions, guarantees, tax liabilities or face value yields, even at the time of the sale.

The only time that disclosure to the consumer is required occurs when the consumer decides to replace an old policy with a new one. Some agents and brokers make a point of finding people with expensive policies and urging their replacement. To make such activity more obvious, and to protect the public from improper replacements, regulations require that the replacing agent supply the client with a completed disclosure form. The form sets out some of the basic facts on both policies in an organized manner, comparing premiums, face amounts, and both coverage and premium durations.

If you read this document you should be able to verify that the new policy is, indeed, better than the old one. However, a copy of the form must be sent to the existing insurance company. This allows the existing insurer to verify that its policy has been accurately described. It also allows the company's "conservation department" to swing into gear and try to reverse the pending loss of one of its policies.

As a consumer, you must be aware that this form will be sent to your old company. While there is no problem in showing the company how its policy is described, this form also shows the complete details of your proposed new policy (except in Ontario, where proposed insurance details are not sent to the existing company). Yet the new policy may be prompted because of very personal or confidential reasons, such as a pending divorce, marriage, business loans, or mergers. This could pose a problem if your old agent was your brother-in-law! Since the disclosure form is routed to the old company's head office, and then back to the branch and agent who originally sold the policy, this personal data will be in the hands of the local branch very quickly. In some provinces, the client used to have the right to request privacy, and stipulate that a copy of the disclosure form not be sent to the existing insurer, but insurance company pressure has caused this small right to privacy to be lost.

Despite this loss of privacy, if you are considering replacing an existing policy, an accurate comparison is very important. This is not easy to do unless the policies are simple and similar. It's easy to compare two five-year term policies, as there are no cash values building to complicate the comparison. It's very difficult to compare a term policy with a whole life policy with dividends. Dividends complicate comparisons because they represent a stream of fluctuating payments. They're often used to buy paid-up additional insurance or to pay for more complicated options. In comparing the cost of two policies, you should assume that future dividends will remain the same as current dividends and assume they are used to reduce the annual premium.

In making the comparison, be sure you are comparing policies of the same duration. Policies can be paid for over a lifetime, by age sixty-five or in as few as ten years. Your agent should have a computer program that can assume different premiums of different durations and apply a rate of interest on the savings. In some cases, there is another factor to be considered if you are contemplating replacement. If you are a smoker and own an old term policy with blended rates – rates that don't distinguish the different life expectancies of smokers and non-smokers – it may very well be better value than a new term policy with smokers' rates.

Policy stripping

A more complex calculation, one that your existing company may not be pleased to illustrate, involves "policy stripping." When you strip an older participating whole life policy, you stop paying the premium and borrow most of the cash value from the policy reserve, leaving just enough cash value to pay the next premium. When you don't mail in a cheque, the insurance company will automatically pay the premium for you with a loan from the policy. If the policy is old enough, the cash value that will build in the policy over the following year will be more than the premium just paid. This sets up the cash value for another similar loan next year, and the year after, and so on. The dividend declared each year should be more than enough to pay the interest on the growing loan.

If you have a participating whole life policy more than fifteen years old, ask the insurance company to illustrate the impact of policy stripping. The company should be able to give you a computer printout that tracks future loans, loan costs and dividend payments. Naturally, the company will warn you that this stripping of the policy will reduce the death benefit. The company will be right. But you will also stop paying premiums, have the use of most of the cash value and still be insured. You might have to be persistent.

Many consumers have old, relatively small whole life policies. When they arrange new, much larger policies, they often decide to cancel the old policies. Stripping is a better choice; you can claim the cash, avoid the premiums and loan interest, yet keep the insurance in force and enjoy some of the protection you've already paid for. Giving the remaining insurance value to your favourite charity, before or after stripping, could furnish you with a tax deduction and provide the charity with a meaningful contribution.

CHAPTER 18

The Rationale for Disability Insurance

WHO WOULD PAY THE BILLS if you were laid up? Your family may be well protected by insurance on your life but would they be exposed to financial hardship if you were unable to work?

It's a risk you shouldn't ignore. There are 3.3 million disabled Canadians; just a few are children. Almost 1.8 million of the disabled are between the ages of fourteen and sixty-four. For most, the disability interferes with the kind and amount of work they're able to do; more than half, 56 percent, have incomes of less than $10,000 a year. As you sit comfortably reading this book, you might find it hard to believe that you could be felled by an illness or an accident. In fact, nearly a third of all people now aged thirty-five will be unable to work for at least six months before reaching age sixty-five. The chances that you'll suffer a disability rather than die before retirement are close to three to one. Put another way, you are five times more likely to become disabled than to die during your working years.

If you were unable to work, where would you get the money to buy food, pay the rent, and look after all your other expenses?

Getting a handle on disability insurance can be frustrating. In terms of life insurance, if you die you collect and if you don't you don't. But what constitutes a disability? It's complicated by definitions, exclusions, occupational classifications, and a raft of options. You're probably already protected by a group disability plan provided by your employer and a mishmash of government and quasi-government plans that might replace your lost income if you become disabled. These plans will pay different amounts of weekly or monthly income under a variety of circumstances. One of the tricky things to grasp about disability insurance is which plans supplement each other and which will not pay a benefit if you are receiving money from another. Another confusion is the tax status

The Likelihood of Suffering a Disability*				
	Likelihood of disability versus death		Average duration of disability in years	
Age	Men	Women	Men	Women
25	3.6 to 1	8.0 to 1	2.2	2.5
35	2.2 to 1	7.1 to 1	3.1	3.4
45	1.4 to 1	4.0 to 1	4.0	4.5
55	1.4 to 1	2.4 to 1	4.6	5.1

*Your chances of suffering a disability compared to your chance of dying before retirement

Note: Based on disability lasting at least ninety days

SOURCE: INSTITUTE OF ACTUARIES

TABLE XIX

of the money you receive – sometimes its taxable, sometimes it's not. Let's look first at government disability protection.

Workers' compensation

All provinces and territories have workers' compensation legislation covering workers in most industries. Workers' comp does not cover entertainers or people who work in some service industries, such as banking and insurance, nor does it cover self-employed people. The benefits are not taxed but your disability must arise from an accident that occurs while on the job or from an occupational disease. Your disability has to be work related; and it's often difficult to tie an illness to work.

You're protected if you suffer from lung disease caused by your work environment but not if you have a heart attack while chatting by the office coffee machine. You won't receive anything from workers' comp if you're disabled in an accident while driving to work, unless you're a travelling salesman.

The benefits for a total disability – defined as the inability to do your own job – differ from province to province. In 1994, you would receive up to $737.88 a week during a temporary disability if you lived in British Columbia. In Ontario, the maximum was $620.77. The boards can also make lump-sum payments if you suffer a permanent disability. Manufacturers and the skilled trades rely on workers' compensation because protection for their employees is very difficult to buy from insurance companies, which like to avoid accident-prone environments. However, accident and sickness and sickness-only group disability policies, discussed later in this chapter, are widely available.

Usually, payments under employer and individual disability plans are integrated with workers' compensation; that is, the income you receive from your disability plans will be reduced by the amount you receive from workers' compensation. Workers' comp coverage begins the day after the accident and continues until you are considered medically fit to return to work.

Unemployment insurance

As well as providing benefits for the jobless, UI pays up to $448 a week (in 1995) for fifteen weeks if you're laid up because of illness or an accident. The benefit is taxable. There's also a two-week waiting period after you've made your claim and you must have medical proof that you can't work at any kind of job – not just your own. To keep the money flowing – even though it's only for a few weeks – you'll have to fill out a UI employment report every two weeks. To qualify for the sickness/accident benefit, you must have worked and contributed to UI through your pay for at least twenty weeks in the last year. The self-employed, who do not pay UI contributions, are not eligible for the UI disability benefit. And, if you are receiving workers' compensation, you cannot claim UI benefits as well.

Many employers contract out of the UI disability benefit, replacing it with their own disability plan. The plans must meet the criteria established by the employment and immigration commission. This results in lower employer and employee UI contributions because the employment and immigration commission is providing a reduced service – jobless benefits but not sickness or accident benefits. You could also enjoy faster payment of benefits through an employer disability plan.

If you receive benefits from both a group plan and UI, the UI benefits will be reduced by the amount you receive from your group plan. To help boost your income while disabled, some group plans are set up to kick in only after the UI benefits run out and sometimes for the two weeks before they start. The plans run by employers to replace the UI disability insurance have several advantages to the employee. They're less cumbersome than UI, more comprehensive, and they pay higher benefits. Finally, if you're laid off after returning to work from a disability, your UI eligibility for unemployment benefits is untouched.

The Canada and Quebec pension plans

You may also be able to turn to the Canada and Quebec pension plans if you find yourself felled by an illness or injury. To qualify, your disability must be "severe and prolonged," and of such a serious nature that you are unable "to pursue gainful employment" of any sort. While the CPP continues this stiff test to age sixty-five, when the CPP retirement benefit kicks in, the QPP relaxes the rule at age sixty. To qualify for the disability benefit at this age, you need only have "a total incapacity to fulfill the requirements of your last job," instead of any job. The disability income you'll receive from CPP/QPP depends on the amount you've contributed to either plan to a maximum, in 1995, of $854.74 a month – and it's taxable.

Meeting the disability qualifications of CPP/QPP is tough; and, unlike the benefits paid by workers' compensation boards, the disability pension is never a partial one. Either you qualify or you don't. However, it's not reduced if you also receive income from a private disability plan. The income you receive from a private disability plan will not change if you start receiving a CPP/QPP benefit; group coverage is usually reduced.

When you begin receiving a CPP/QPP disability benefit, your child or children will receive $161.27 a month in 1995 from the CPP, $50.95 under the QPP. (If your child is under eighteen years old, the cheque will be sent to the person with custody of the child.) The income will continue until the child reaches age eighteen, or up to age twenty-five if attending school full-time. A child who has lost the earning power of both CPP-contributing parents through disability can claim two child benefits.

Auto insurance

If you're injured in an auto accident and unable to work, you might be able to claim income-replacement benefits from your auto insurance policy. The amount you can claim varies from province to province; the benefit is not taxable. The benefits are outlined in your auto insurance policy, whether the insurance system in your province is privately or publicly run. Even where it's private, as in Ontario, the provisions of the policy are dictated by provincial regulations.

Any benefit from your auto insurance policy will not affect your UI benefit. However, your group insurance will kick in first, with your auto insurance sometimes providing a top-up after all other benefits are paid.

Victims of crime

All provinces and territories have programs for compensating victims of crime. In some, there are separate criminal injuries compensation boards; in others, the victim compensation system is part of the workers' compensation board. The compensation benefits paid vary. In Ontario, for example, the Criminal Injuries Compensation Board awards maximum one-time payments of $25,000 and periodic payments of up to $1,000 a month.

Generally, the victim compensation systems are little known to the public, so if you are injured in a mugging or other criminal act, be sure to find out what you are entitled to in your province. Look in the provincial/territorial government section of your phone book.

Group disability insurance

Although government and auto insurance create a safety net, there are too many holes in the protection to provide real security. The disability income from workers' compensation is generous but you're not likely to be disabled by an accident or illness caused at work. Unemployment insurance and CPP or QPP are less generous and more restrictive. The foundation of your disability protection is probably a group plan.

Short-term: At the end of 1992, more than 1.9 million Canadian employees were covered by short-term disability group policies; another 5.9 million were protected by long-term disability plans. Many of these plans are provided by employers as a company benefit, but unions and professional associations are also becoming involved in group disability.

Short-term disability plans usually pay a weekly benefit for seventeen to twenty-six weeks from the date of the disability. Less commonly, the benefits can last for as long as fifty-two weeks. A typical plan uses the 1-8-26 formula: Benefits begin on the first day of an employee's disability if hurt in an accident but eight days after being struck down by sickness. Disability payments would last up to twenty-six weeks. Most group insurance policies cover disabilities arising from accidents and illnesses with only three exceptions: self-inflicted injuries, acts of war, and normal pregnancy. (If there are complications to a pregnancy that oblige a woman to take extra time off work, she is protected.) However, a few policies exclude disabilities caused by accidents or hazards at work. These are called non-occupation policies; employers with these policies assume a disability arising from work will be covered by workers' compensation. Occasionally, a policy will restrict benefits if the person disabled is suffering from a mental or nervous disorder, or the disability is caused by a pre-existing condition.

Long-term: Benefits from most long-term group plans usually kick in after six months, although a few plans have only a three-month waiting period. There are a couple of plans that will make you wait a year. Most group plans will pay a disability income until you reach age sixty-five. Many employer short-term disability plans have been replaced by cumulative sick-pay plans. These plans allow an employee a set number of "sick days," typically twenty, in a year. Sick-pay plans have a built-in incentive not to take unnecessary time off work because unused sick days are "banked" and can be at least partly "withdrawn" at retirement in cash or time.

Group disability plans have strengths and weaknesses. If your company has a plan, you may be entitled to coverage without evidence of insurability. (It can be difficult for individuals to buy disability coverage; insurance companies are quick to reject anyone who might be a poor risk.) On the other hand, the circumstances in which your group plan considers you to be disabled could be so restrictive you will likely never receive a benefit; but, if you do qualify, most company plans will pay a disability benefit until you're sixty-five years old. Most company plans will pay a benefit if you're unable to work at your usual occupation. Often, this is the definition for the first two years of your disability. After that, you will be considered disabled if you can't perform any work for which you have the education, training or experience. A few insurers will cut off your benefits as soon as you can do any kind of work.

Also, as with most disability plans, your benefits will reflect your income at the time you are disabled. However, group plans seldom provide protection against inflation. Your benefits in the first year may be adequate but if you were to be disabled for a long time you would soon begin to feel the pinch. A few group plans have a cost-of-living allowance, but usually you have to buy it as a rider.

Most plans are guaranteed renewable but the future premiums are not; the cost of your plan could skyrocket. Also, you'll lose your coverage if you lose your job or change employers; some employers will suspend your protection if you're on strike.

Paying your own disability premiums

The disability income from group plans varies widely; it can run between 50 and 70 percent of your income, less the benefits paid by unemployment insurance or any other plan. There's a ceiling, typically of $2,500 to $3,000 a month. A few generous employers will top it up so that you will be receiving your full pay for a few months. If your employer has paid all, or even a small share, of the disability insurance premiums, the income you will receive if disabled will be taxable (we'll come to the exception in a moment); it will not be taxable if you've paid the premiums yourself. While it may be to your advantage if your employer pays the premiums while you're working, the consequences will be a tax on your benefits if you are disabled. It's hard enough to make ends meet on a reduced income; paying taxes would make it that much tougher.

Employers who recognize the benefits to their employees of not paying the insurance premiums out of the corporate kitty often try to make up for it by paying all the premiums on life, dental and supplemental health insurance policies. Employers should be wary; Revenue Canada is clamping down on employee-paid disability policies. It has decided that if the employer pays any of the cost of maintaining the plans, the benefits become taxable to the employees. Such costs could include administration; claims handling; legal, actuarial, and consulting fees; or any other costs of establishing, operating, or winding-up of the plans.

Because of this situation, The Alexander Consulting Group, an employee benefits consulting firm, advised employers in mid-1990: "In future, these costs should be identified and funded by employee contributions in order to maintain the tax-free status of the benefits." In an advisory letter, the firm continued: "Surplus funds from one plan are used sometimes to subsidize another plan. Revenue Canada has warned that cross-subsidization could also taint an employee-pay-all plan. Even in the absence of actual subsidies, if the level of benefits, premium rates or other terms assume the availability of common resources, the employee-pay-all plan could be tainted.

"Although this new position by Revenue Canada has not been tested in the courts, it would be prudent for plan sponsors to safeguard the tax-free nature of benefits by reviewing and, if necessary, modifying their practices in this area."

There is an exception to the rule that plan benefits are taxable if an employer pays any part of long-term group disability premiums. This little-known exception has resulted in the refund by Revenue Canada of many thousands of dollars. George Brett first wrote about this tax quirk in his column in *The Toronto Star* in 1983. A Revenue Canada interpretation bulletin explains that disability benefits that would otherwise be taxable as income will not be taxed if they were received from a plan that existed on June 18, 1971, and the disability arose from an "event" that occurred before 1974.

The interpretation bulletin, IT-428, available from Revenue Canada district taxation offices, explains that the pre-1974 "event" could be an injury or the identification of a degenerative disease. As long as group disability plans that existed on June 18, 1971, are still in force, the income to qualifying recipients remains non-taxable. If you think you might qualify, get a copy of IT-428 and read it carefully. Write a letter explaining the situation to the Revenue Canada taxation centre that processes your return. The addresses are in the appendix. You will be contacted and asked to provide medical proof and documentation from your employer. Don't expect quick results; six to eight months seems to be the average. You're not allowed to claim tax rebates going back more than three years. If you do indeed qualify for tax-free treatment of your disability income, you will not only be pocketing the refund but also ensuring that your future disability income is not taxed.

Richer benefits for women on maternity leave

Two 1989 court rulings in Canada have resulted in improved benefits for women on maternity leave from their jobs. In May of that year, the Supreme Court of Canada gave a major boost to women's rights in the workplace in ruling that sexual discrimination includes unfair treatment on the basis of pregnancy. In reversing its own previous ruling of eleven years earlier, the court ruled: "Pregnancy discrimination is a form of sex discrimination simply because of the basic biological fact that only women have the capacity to become pregnant." The case was initiated by three Manitoba women who were denied short-term company disability benefits by their employer when they were pregnant and receiving unemployment insurance benefits. As a result of the ruling, many short-term disability plans across Canada have been altered to improve benefits for women on maternity leave.

CHAPTER 19

Shopping for a Disability Policy

AFTER READING THE CHAPTER on government, auto and group disability insurance, you may conclude that they would not do an adequate job of protecting your income if you were disabled. The well-heeled – executives, doctors, lawyers – might find the benefit from their group plan would scarcely put a dent in their living expenses. Then there are the self-employed who don't qualify for membership in an association that offers a group disability policy.

These people can buy the protection they need through individual long-term disability policies, which cover 665,000 Canadians. Such a policy can be the foundation of your protection or it can just top up the group protection you already have. Unlike life insurance, your disability coverage will not be determined by your family's need but by your income and the ceiling imposed by the insurance company. At the time you buy the policy, the company will take into consideration the benefits you would receive from other disability plans. It would then agree to pay you a monthly benefit that would bring your disability income up to no more than 70 percent of your working income. In general, you can't pile one benefit on top of another to end up with a higher income than you would earn if you were at work. The insurers are willing to ensure you can cover your necessities of life but they're not going to make your life so comfortable you would be hesitant to return to work. Those with incomes exceeding $400,000 or $500,000 could receive as little as 25 percent of their working income. The proportion of coverage decreases as income increases.

The cost of your coverage is complicated by the kind of policy and the various options you choose. Overall, the cost of your policy will climb with the likelihood that the insurer will have to pay if you're disabled; the better the protection, the more you'll have to pay. The premiums will also depend on your age and occupation. Disability insurers classify workers according to the risk in their jobs.

The likelihood that you will eventually collect on your disability policy has made the insurance companies very wary in recent years. You will be questioned on your hobbies, work habits and lifestyle. The insurance companies are experiencing heavy claims for disabilities arising from stress, nervous breakdowns, and drug or alcohol abuse; they've become cautious about insuring applicants who admit to working long hours and never taking vacations.

Although every company offers a range of policies, most insurers specialize in covering different segments of the working population. Your life insurance agent or broker will know or be able to find out which company will offer you the best protection. In choosing the policies offered to you, you'll be expected to tailor your coverage to your own need for protection. There are, in fact, only two criteria you should demand without swaying. Make sure your policy is non-cancellable and guaranteed renewable. You want to make sure your insurer can't cancel your coverage or raise your premiums as long as you pay them.

The remaining details will have to be established by you. Let's go through them one by one.

What is a disability?

When you're looking for disability protection, you have to know what the policy means by the term "disability." This is the policy's "disability definition" and you should read it carefully. Don't hear only what you want to hear – that you'll be paid if you're off work because of an injury or sickness. You might not be. There are three common definitions of disability:

"Own occupation" or "regular occupation": Disability is sometimes defined as the inability to perform the duties of your usual job. This is called an "own occupation" or "regular occupation" definition. Thus, a sales agent who developed a mental disorder that impaired his ability to deal with the public would be considered disabled, even if he was working full time in some other job. These policies are well suited to those occupations that demand special education or experience and are sensitive to even minor health problems. Surgeons would be considered disabled if they developed a nervous tremor; airline pilots would be able to collect benefits if they suffered an eye injury. On the other hand, an accountant could lose an eye, a hand, or a foot and still work as hard as ever. Some companies add the phrase "and not otherwise gainfully employed." These few words significantly water down the protection. Some companies add "one or more of the essential duties of your regular occupation." These words add strength to the definition.

"Any occupation": Some policies will consider you to be disabled only if you are unable to work at any job for which you are qualified by education, training or experience. This is an "any occupation" definition.

"Total disability": The shallowest protection is from a policy that considers you disabled only if you're unable to work at all. This definition is seldom found in private insurance plans.

The disability definition is the key to the quality of your plan; it will determine whether or not you'll receive a disability benefit if you're not able to work. Not only should you read it carefully, but you should also look at the time period during which the definition is in effect. Some policies will use the "own occupation" definition for the first two years but will continue to pay benefits only if you qualify under the "any occupation" definition after that time.

Make sure your policy will pay benefits whether your disability arises from accidents or illness. Some will protect you only from disabling injuries and not illness. A few, called non-occupational policies, exclude disabilities that arise from the hazards of work on the assumption you'll be protected by workers' compensation. You want a policy that will cover disability, whatever the cause. There are a few exclusions you can't avoid; you are not protected if your disability arises from war or normal pregnancy. Some policies exclude self-inflicted injuries yet many accidents could be considered "self-inflicted." There are policies that even exclude claims that arise from alcohol or drug abuse, very common causes of disability. Avoid any policy that won't pay for mental or nervous disorders.

Will you receive a benefit if you're working part-time?
Traditionally, you'll be paid a benefit only if you stop working completely. If you return to work part-time your cheques will stop. It's a scenario that doesn't really match your needs; it makes it awkward for you to return to work gradually, building your strength as you lengthen the hours you can work without damaging your

health. Under the terms of your insurance, once you're back to your "own occupation," the disability cheques will stop appearing in the mail – even though your income is reduced. This doesn't benefit the insurance companies either, which would rather see you back at work.

As a better alternative, the insurance companies have added residual or partial disability riders to their "own occupation" or "any occupation" policies. They also sell residual policies, which have an "own" or "any" occupation definition of disability. Under these policies, you'll be paid a benefit that matches the percentage of your lost income as a percentage of your full disability benefit. Not only does the penalty for returning to work disappear, but also there can be a significant financial reward. Often your income while partially disabled – made up of your earnings from work plus your disability benefits – will be higher than your disability benefits if you stayed home. With a residual benefit, you're encouraged to go back to work as soon as you feel able. It's a win-win situation. You return to work as soon as you can without fear that benefits will be cut off, and the insurer pays partial benefits for a period when you might have stayed home to avoid the cutoff.

A "residual" policy insures your income level, rather than your occupation. If your income drops, the policy pays a benefit in proportion to the loss. If your income drops by 50 percent, the policy will pay 50 percent of the income insured. A full disability benefit would be paid if your income was cut by 75 to 80 percent. There are small differences in the formulas used by insurers to determine loss of earnings for establishing your residual benefits. The insurers might look only at your best six consecutive months in the past eighteen or your best year of the last three. Under a basic residual policy, you would be expected to accept any work you're capable of performing; a residual policy with an "own" occupation rider would pay full benefits so long as you had not returned to your usual job, even if you were working at a different kind of job.

Sometimes people can lose a limb, their vision, or their hearing and still be able to work. Policies with a presumptive disability provision would pay a benefit, even if your income was unscathed.

Residual or presumptive benefits are not available from every company for every occupation classification. Generally, blue-collar workers will have trouble getting residual benefits, while their white-collar colleagues won't.

In the past, you had to be fully disabled before you could claim a residual benefit. If your doctor wanted to prevent a serious illness and warned you to slow down, perhaps work only a few days a week, you would not be eligible for a benefit. This was seen to be unfair – and potentially more expensive for the insurance companies. Now some insurers will let you claim a partial benefit without any "partial disability qualification period."

When will your benefit kick in?
After you are injured or fall ill, the waiting period before you begin receiving benefits can range from two weeks to two years. This is called the "elimination period." If it's only a few weeks or a month, your policy will be more expensive than if you're willing to wait longer for the benefits to start; insurance companies know that even if you suffer a heart attack you could be back at work within three to six months. If you have group disability insurance, it makes sense to time your individual coverage to begin when the group coverage ends, or plan to have your own insurance increase when group coverage ends.

The cost of disability insurance drops dramatically with the longer elimination period. If the insurance premiums are too costly for your budget, increase your elimination period rather than accept less than all the disability protection available. If a thirty-five-year-old non-smoking man bought a policy that would pay a $2,000-a-month benefit to age sixty-five, he would pay about $1,478 if he chooses a thirty-day elimination period. His premiums would drop to $1,080 if he opted for an elimination period of sixty days, $949 for a ninety-day wait and $1,912 for a 120-day wait.

How long will your benefit last?
Individual long-term disability policies provide benefits that continue anywhere from two years from the start of the disability to a lifetime. The most common are two years, five years, to age sixty-five, and for life. Don't buy a policy with anything less than benefits to age sixty-five. It costs little more than a five-year benefit policy yet if a disability was to linger for five years, it will probably last for the rest of your life. A lifetime benefit is best.

Will your benefits keep pace with inflation?
Some insurers have guaranteed increases in your coverage built into their policy, so that coverage increases by a small amount each year to keep pace with your rising income. Others provide for more

coverage but you have to apply for it. Of course, your insurance premium will rise along with the coverage and you must prove that your income has increased in order to justify the higher coverage.

This will ensure that the first benefit cheque you receive after becoming disabled will meet your needs. To ensure that your disability income will also keep pace with the cost of living after you are disabled, you will have to buy a cost-of-living allowance, or COLA, rider to your disability policy. This rider provides that after you have been collecting benefits for a year, the benefits will increase each year in line with the Consumer Price Index or at a fixed annual percentage increase. For anyone younger than fifty, a COLA rider is a must. If you were disabled, inflation could destroy the value of a fixed disability income.

Sometimes your working income will rise faster than the rate of inflation, especially if you're young and just launching your career. The guaranteed future insurability option will give you the right to buy additional coverage in future at standard rates for your age and occupation, despite any degeneration in your health. There will be limits but this can be a valuable option, especially for a young professional who might start at $40,000 a year on graduation from university but be earning more than $100,000 within a few years. Disability insurance is underwritten far more carefully than life insurance, and it is relatively easy to lose your insurability. An ailment as simple as a kidney stone can make you uninsurable. If you believe you might need the extra coverage and can arrange it now, lock it in.

How about recurring disabilities?

If you recover from a disability and return to work, the benefits usually stop. If you have a relapse, you may have to go through another waiting period before your disability benefit resumes. Some policies have a recurrent disability clause that protects you against this problem. Each insurer is different, but usually, if your second loss of earnings from the same cause occurs within six to twelve months of your return to work, it will be treated as a continuation of the first. The normal waiting period is then waived.

Disability insurance innovations

Disability insurance has been sold in Canada for nearly thirty years but it's been a tough sell for the insurance companies. In recent years, a few companies have added interesting wrinkles to their policies to make them more attractive. Several disability insurance companies in Canada offer "retirement protector" and "future savings protector" policies. The rationale is that disability benefits are intentionally kept meagre to encourage you to return to work; often this means you have to dip into your savings just to pay your daily expenses. A disability of even brief duration can shatter your retirement savings plans. In addition, without any earned income, you can't contribute to an RRSP. The retirement policies safeguard your retirement by contributing up to $1,000 a month to a trust account while you are disabled. The benefit is paid into a self-directed trust fund and held until paid out as a lump sum when you're sixty-five. If you're already protected by a group or individual policy, you can buy the retirement protector as a distinct policy or as a rider.

Canada Life has an option that returns 85 percent of your premiums after ten years if you've never had to claim a benefit. If you keep the policy in force for another eight years, 85 percent of the premiums will be returned to you again. Other companies offer similar arrangements.

There are also policies that have been created to meet the particular needs of the owners and managers of small businesses or professional practices. There are policies that will pay any income tax that might be due, for example those arising from a deferred year-end. There are other policies that will cover fixed business expenses such as rent, salaries and office overhead; another policy will pick up the interest and principal on a business loan; and yet another will pay the salary of your replacement to keep the business afloat. A few insurance companies have life insurance policies that will pay a lump sum if you suffer a heart attack, stroke or cancer, even if you don't die. These are "living benefits," discussed in chapter thirteen. Usually, buy-sell agreements cover only the death of a major shareholder with life insurance; these disability riders can be used to pay the disabled shareholder for his or her shares. If the benefits are paid to the business they'll be tax-free; if they're paid to the shareholder they'll be taxable.

Finally, the insurance companies are still tussling with unisex rates for men and women. Disability insurers used to quote separately for men and women, with men's rates lower than those for women. Paul Revere introduced unisex rates in 1984 and most of the other companies followed. In 1990, however, Revere returned to separate rates, with men's rates again somewhat lower than those for women. Women shopping for disability insurance might be able to get a better deal with a company still offering unisex rates.

Some insurers have introduced the "group offset rider" to meet the needs of high-income individuals who have employee disability plans that will not pay sufficient benefits to meet their needs. The terms of these riders vary from company to company but they all aim to provide full coverage. Let's look at an example: A forty-five-year-old non-smoking man earns $200,000 a year and pays all of the premiums for his group plan. If he is disabled, he'll receive his benefits tax-free. But the plan pays only 60 percent of his income to a maximum of $5,000 a month. This would probably not be enough for him if he was disabled for a long period of time, especially since very few group plans are indexed to inflation.

He has three choices. He can "top up" his group plan with a private plan to the maximum that the company will allow. An insurance company would issue an additional $1,325 a month for total coverage of $6,325. This additional coverage would cost about $1,100 annually for a fully indexed plan with all the essential benefits. His second choice would be to drop the group coverage altogether (if permitted by the employer) and substitute his own private coverage, also to the limit of $6,325. The cost for full private coverage would be about $5,075 a year.

The third alternative, somewhat of an innovation in the industry, is the group offset rider. In this case, the existing group insurance is "peeled back" and the private coverage placed under it. The full $6,325 is applied for but the executive receives a discount of about $250 for the existing group insurance.

What is the advantage of the group offset rider when the group plan will be paying most of the benefit? Although it looks like an expensive way to top up with $1,325 monthly coverage, there are several advantages. The automatic indexing is based on the full $6,325 and this will be added each year. If the client leaves his place of employment, he has $6,325 of personally owned disability insurance instead of only $1,325. If and when the group insurance stops paying, perhaps at age sixty-five, or because of a weak definition of disability, the private plan picks up the difference with a lifetime benefit period. It's an expensive solution but it does plug the holes.

Another recent innovation is temporary coverage for terminated or "out-placed" employees. Sadly, this has been an increasing phenomenon; an employee who has only employer-sponsored group insurance cannot take it with him on termination of employment. Since he or she does not have any income to insure, disability insurers will not issue a policy. Although few life agents or brokers have access to this temporary coverage, there are a couple of companies that will provide temporary coverage if action is taken immediately upon or after termination. Clearly, this would not be necessary if you already have the group offset type of disability insurance in place.

Protection by mail

Back in 1984, the Ontario Superintendent of Insurance issued a statement that has stood the test of time. "You get what you pay for," the Superintendent said after his office had received a flood of complaints from consumers who had bought low-cost disability insurance sold door-to-door, through newspaper advertisements, or by mail throughout Ontario and Canada.

"These consumers later discovered that the policies offered only very limited coverage" and, in particular, did not cover illness. "Generally, these policies provide full payouts only for disability resulting from accidents of a restricted or unusual nature, such as a public transit mishap." The Superintendent advised: "Disability policies better suited to the needs of many people can be obtained through a workplace group, or as individual policies directly from an insurance company."

The advice is as relevant today as it was then. Be extremely wary about what a policy does not cover. Some companies will not pay benefits for drug and alcohol abuse, or mental disorders. Yet substance abuse and mental problems are major causes of long-term disability.

Then there are hospital cash plans, which pay only while you're confined to hospital. Others pay only in the case of accidents – yet the vast majority of disabilities are caused by illness. Credit card balance and line-of-credit disability insurance are not desirable because they don't take your occupation into consideration. Because they don't, they're based on the highest risk occupation – blue-collar work – and are very expensive.

Shopping tips

Too few people are protected by disability insurance; it's confusing and expensive. All of the options are nice to have – just like a car loaded with all the extras – but in buying disability insurance you will also run up against the affordability barrier. Look for insurance that is non-cancellable (by the insurance company, except for non-payment of premium) and protects you from any kind of disability, whether it arises from an accident or an illness.

You should buy as much coverage as you possibly can, a residual benefit, benefits to at least age sixty-five and cost of living protection. Such a policy will do a good job of protecting your income. Only you can decide whether you want to buy an "own occupation" policy rather than an "any occupation" policy; the answer lies in the fragility of your work skills as well as your willingness to switch occupations if financially necessary. After looking at your own financial cushion and the protection you have with the government or group plans, decide whether you want your benefits to start within weeks or months of being disabled. Remember you can keep your premiums lower by choosing a longer waiting period.

It's not difficult to shop for disability insurance. There are only a few companies selling individual coverage in the Canadian marketplace – a market dominated by Paul Revere Life Insurance Co., with just under 40 percent of the market (in 1991), Great-West Life Assurance Co., with close to 25 percent, and Provident Life & Accident Insurance Co. You can call the Canadian Life and Health Insurance Association for a complete list of companies which offer long-term non-cancellable individual disability insurance in Canada.

A personal experience with disability insurance

Since the above chapter was written, I have been disabled from work because of depression. Interestingly, this depression was a result of my reaction to my treatment by a general insurance company – but that's another story. After selling and promoting disability insurance for twenty years, it has been most informative to see the insurance from a consumer's – and claimant's – point of view.

I owned a $2,000-a-month policy with Unum, based on an old "own occupation" definition of disability. According to this definition, as long as I was unable to work as an insurance broker (my occupation), the company would pay me benefits of $2,000 a month.

I also own a $6,000-a-month policy with Canada Life. This is a residual policy, which pays in proportion to my lost income from disability. Since my earned income fell by over 80 percent, this policy has paid me the full amount monthly. The policy contains a cost-of-living clause that has slowly increased the payments from $6,000 a month to almost $8,000.

Neither policy has responded as smoothly as I expected, nor have the issuing companies treated me as I would want one of my own clients to be treated. Although I'm sure that this is not the case, I have the feeling that I must be the only significant claim on Canada Life's books. From time to time, the company has forgotten to mail my cheque. My phone calls are greeted with responses like "Oh – we forgot to write the cheque. Your file is over in the legal department. Come over tomorrow and we will have it ready for you."

When disabled, without one's regular income and totally dependent on disability benefits, self-esteem and confidence are already in the gutter. At such a time, it is disconcerting to think that a battery of corporate lawyers is trying to find a way out of paying your claim.

Financially, Canada Life has come through for me. The claim manager has been honest and professional and, on balance, the policy has performed as promised and as advertised. In fact, when I was diagnosed as suffering from depression, Canada Life determined that this condition had existed for six months and I was awarded a gratuitous initial payment of $40,000.

My experience with Unum began as a straightforward claim, with a monthly cheque for $2,000 being issued through a computerized system. I was asked for an annual statement of my health, together with a report from my doctor. After seven years of claims, an investigator was sent to visit me. I was told that since I was going to my office, I was not entitled to benefits. According to the policy, I was considered totally disabled if I could not perform the duties of my own occupation. I am an insurance broker but am currently working in my own company as an insurance clerk, at a wage of one-tenth my old income. The investigator reported that I should be cut off from receiving benefits.

I was cut off, despite the fact that my physician believed that I am still depressed and unable to perform my old duties, and that attempting to do so might jeopardize my recovery. Unum stopped paying benefits without asking my attending physician for a report of my health. I protested and was offered an evaluating visit from the company's own doctor. This struck me as a backward, "shoot-first" reaction since my benefit payments had already been halted. I eventually retained a lawyer.

Unum's lawyer quickly agreed to pay me the lost benefits for approximately one year and to buy back the policy for $50,000. Since I no longer had faith in the protection offered by the policy, this seemed like a good idea.

Recently, I received a letter from Unum advising me that my policy was terminated. I had yet to receive any money, nor had I signed an agreement surrendering the policy. To my knowledge, the company had no authority to terminate my policy since it was a guaranteed non-cancellable contract. Shortly after this, a settlement cheque for $75,000 was received by my lawyer's office on my behalf. The cheque has since been twice rejected for non-sufficient funds.

During my disability, a client, a surgeon who accidentally crushed his foot and was unable to work for a short time, also had a less-than-satisfying experience with Unum. I have recommended Unum to clients in the past and am now very concerned for the value of their protection. In response to my calls to the Ontario Insurance Commission, I have been advised that the commission does not get involved in claim disputes.

I have practiced what I preached. I recommended disability insurance and covered my own risks. Without adequate protection, I might not be alive today. My advice? Deal with an insurance agent or broker who can assure you that he or she has had satisfactory claims experience with the company being proposed.

CHAPTER 20

How Safe Is Your Money?

LIFE INSURANCE COMPANIES are subject to strict solvency requirements, set out in law and overseen by the federal and provincial governments. Each government regulates the solvency of the companies it has incorporated, while Ottawa has exclusive jurisdiction over the solvency of foreign companies operating in Canada with branch offices. This safety is enhanced by the fact that life insurance companies invest heavily in approved securities meeting exacting quality standards, such as government long-term bonds.

The Canadian life insurance industry used to boast that no one has ever lost a cent through failure of insurance companies in Canada to honour their obligations. Just the same, in 1990, after a wave of concern that followed the failure of two Alberta banks, the industry created a consumer protection plan designed to safeguard policyholders against loss of benefits should a member company become insolvent or go out of business. The plan, which covers contracts issued before it went into effect as well as after, provides insurance for your insurance.

Through the Canadian Life and Health Insurance Compensation Corp., or CompCorp, the plan provides free compensation to each person covered of:

• Up to $200,000 (in death benefits) per life insured per company.

• A lump sum of up to $60,000 for each person who chooses to cash in a registered retirement savings plan or registered retirement income fund.

• A one-time option to owners of registered retirement income funds and cashable annuities to forgo the $60,000 cash withdrawal compensation in return for a life annuity insured for up to $2,000 a month.

• Up to $2,000 a month for someone already receiving income from a non-cashable life annuity or disability income policy.

Apart from the strict solvency requirements and CompCorp, Canadians can't always rely on law and regulation to protect them. Life insurance buyers should always be aware of where their legal protection is solid and where there are gaps.

In 1991, CompCorp responded to the collapse of Les Cooperants Mutual Life Society, a Quebec-chartered life insurance company. Although the protection limit to policyholders was a maximum of $200,000 for life insurance and $60,000 for annuities and RRSPs, CompCorp elected to fully protect all policyholders. The other insurance companies in Canada have been assessed a share of this cost as this is how CompCorp is funded.

Such a generous offer is unlikely to be repeated and consumers should not assume that their policies are 100 percent protected nor that they are safe with any company.

In the first edition of this book, we said that no one had ever lost a dollar with a Canadian life insurance company. Since then, each successive edition has been edited to include comments about yet another life insurance company that had been declared insolvent. What can we learn from these experiences?

First, the collapse of each company has been preceded by warning signs. A vigilant consumer or broker might very well be able to recognize the warning signs, and bail out. The root cause of all three collapses has been management failure. Confederation Life Insurance Company invested so heavily in real estate-related assets, including commercial real estate and mortgages, that a 5 percent drop in values would have wiped out all of their reserves. When the recession hit Southern Ontario, Confederation Life was probably doomed.

Your first source of information is an insurance broker. Brokers represent more than one company, ranking them on the quality of service, the cost of their insurance and the personalities of those with whom they have to deal. After the collapse of Confederation Life, there can be no doubt that financial strength will be a ranking consideration, if it was not before. Insurance company finances and financial requirements are very complex – far beyond the scope of the training of your broker. Therefore, his or her opinion will be based on the reports of rating agencies such as Moody's, Standard & Poor's and A.M. Best (all American companies) or TRAC Insurance Services Ltd. (a Canadian company). TRAC publishes an annual evaluation of all the life companies licenced in Canada. It accurately reported the financial difficulty of Sovereign and Confederation at least a year before they collapsed. The role of the regulator is different in Canada than in the United States. For this reason, the American rating companies may not be as useful as a Canadian service in identifying a company in difficulty.

We can hope that the regulators will also learn from the Confed Life fiasco; perhaps they'll begin to step in a little earlier to take control of failing companies so that clients do not face a loss. In the meantime, here are some guidelines to protect your assets.

First, demand that your broker consider the company's strength when recommending an insurer. He or she has many companies from which to choose and can make a point of recommending one of the stronger ones. The recommendation should be in writing. Ask to see a third-party evaluation of the recommended company. Keep in mind that size is not a guarantee of solvency. Confederation Life was one of Canada's largest life companies.

Second, the insurer will not insure you without first asking a number of personal health and financial questions; it's your right to ask a few questions too.

Third, don't forget to follow up once in a while to make sure that your company remains well-regarded. Should you wish to check the viability of an insurer, TRAC will send you a "Life Line," a detailed financial report of the company. This can be ordered by calling (416) 363-6103.

Fourth, don't be afraid to split your insurance between companies or owners to remain within the limitations of your CompCorp protection. Instead of buying a single $500,000 policy, for example, you could buy two $250,000 policies. Or you could buy two $250,000 policies from the same company but you will own one while your spouse owns the second. You can also split your RRSPs among institutions. This strategy reduces your risk for a small increase in cost, about $75 a year in additional administration costs.

Your best protection is to be fussy about the quality of the company you choose. TRAC rates companies on eight different financial tests. You could reasonably insist that your company have passed at least six of eight tests for each of the last five years.

If you buy policies with questionable companies, but keep coverage down to the CompCorp insured limits, you face two risks. First, you have no guarantee that CompCorp will continue with its current coverage. They might very well change to a co-insurance sys-

Disclosure statement for proposed life insurance

INSURANCE COMPANY_____

Name of policy owner _____

Name of insured _____

Name of beneficiary _____

FACE AMOUNT (payable at death)_____

YES	NO	
☐	☐	Guaranteed
☐	☐	Level until death
☐	☐	Application subject to company approval

INITIAL PREMIUM $ _____   per year

              or $ _____   per month

This premium applicable for _____ years, or for life.

YES	NO	
☐	☐	This and future premiums guaranteed
☐	☐	Level
☐	☐	Non-smoker's rate

OTHER BENEFITS   Guaranteed?   Yes ☐   No ☐

Cash value at age _____ $ _____ or in _____ years.

Policy paid up (premiums cease) at age _____ or in _____ years.

Convertible without medical evidence until age _____ .

Date:_____   I acknowledge receipt of this disclosure:

_____   _____

Broker or agent   Signature of applicant

I certify that policy number _____ hereby delivered, conforms to the

description above, without change or exception

Broker or agent:_____ Date:_____

TABLE XX

tem, where a stipulated percentage of loss is your responsibility. Buying several policies with poor companies might, in effect, maximize your potential loss.

Provincial governments regulate all matters of contract – premium rates, advertising, the wording of contracts, and similar matters – through an insurance act that controls the distribution of insurance. Some provinces then regulate insurance directly, while others delegate this day-to-day responsibility to insurance councils made up of representatives of government and insurance companies and brokers.

Regulations on what agents must disclose to you, the consumer, are weak or nonexistent. While the securities industry requires full disclosure of all relevant information before you buy a new security, the life industry can sell life insurance, even universal life insurance containing investment reserves controlled by the policyholder, without disclosing any material information. Regulations do not require disclosure of future premiums, deductions or guarantees at the time of sale unless the policy is to replace an existing one.

The Independent Life Insurance Brokers of Canada, an association of independent life agents and brokers, has suggested a solution to this problem. It wants each insurance company to develop a description of each of its current and past products. These descriptions would be written in a common format, briefly describing premiums, coverage, cash values, taxation and guarantees. A description would be included with each new policy sold, and a copy would be mailed for each existing policy.

This sort of full disclosure at the time of sale would ensure that the consumer has the facts to understand all the relevant aspects of a new policy. This would be in contrast to current practice, where the consumer has to figure out what questions to ask, and then hope that the agent is knowledgeable and tells the whole truth.

Under the brokers' proposal, the consumer would be required to sign a form indicating that he or she is in possession of the required description of the policy; if a replacement policy is being sold, the consumer would have to have a description of both the old policy and the new. This would allow a better understanding of the true nature of a policy at the time of purchase. It would also assure life companies that their policies are being correctly described, since they would write their own descriptions. Finally, it would permit a consumer to compare two policies without having to disclose personal plans to an existing insurer.

Ontario has adopted this proposal, and regulations have been drafted that require the agent or broker to disclose relevant information about a proposed policy, in writing, at the time of application. An illustration of the disclosure form developed by the Independent Life Insurance Brokers Association of Canada for its Ontario members can be found on page 144. If you are applying for insurance in any province, ask the agent to provide this basic information with his or her signature. In addition to the gaps in insurance regulation mentioned above, most provinces do not require agents to protect the public by having insurance against errors and omissions. One of the first questions you should ask the person who proposes to sell you insurance is whether he or she can give you this personal protection. Once again, in Ontario the proposal has been adopted and agents here must have insurance covering errors and omissions.

Safeguarding your insurance

There are also steps you can take to protect yourself. Most of this book is devoted to helping you choose the right insurance in the right amounts for your family's protection. After taking all that trouble, you don't want the money to end up in the wrong hands.

Every policy specifies who will receive the death benefit. It can state "estate of the insured" or name a specific person, such as "Valerie Smith, wife of the insured," or a group of people, "the children of the insured," or a company.

If the life insurance is to protect your family, you should probably name your spouse as beneficiary, rather than your estate or children. When you die, your estate has a legal responsibility to pay your bills, loans and taxes, and even respond to legal actions. You might have died in an accident for which others hold you liable, and for which your estate might be sued. In this case, if your life insurance was payable to your estate, the money could be tied up for years. It is even possible that your family might receive nothing.

On the other hand, your spouse is not obliged to use insurance death benefits to pay your debts and obligations, though normally this is done. Life insurance proceeds are virtually creditor-proof. The courts have agreed that the family cannot be sued for the insurance money while the estate can.

As for leaving insurance benefits to children, this can create more problems than it solves, unless your spouse is financially secure. A minor is not allowed to receive the funds, so the money would be held in trust – an expense and a complication. We suggest the life insurance should not be left to a child unless there are special circumstances, and a lawyer has been consulted. Parents of a handicapped child might very well have such a special circumstance.

CHAPTER 21

Making an Insurance Claim

INSURANCE COMPANIES TAKE pride in the fact that the beneficiaries of life insurance policies can claim a death benefit without the help of a lawyer or other expert. A phone call to any agent or branch office of the company will produce a list of requirements. Typically, these will be:

1) A birth certificate or other proof of age for the insured. This is to prove that the proper premium has been paid on the policy over the years. If an error in age is discovered, the company will refund any excess premium (if the deceased's age was less than the company understood it to be) or reduce the death benefit (if the age was greater). The same would apply if the company had misunderstood the insured's gender. (Men are charged higher premiums than women the same age because they are likely to die sooner.)

2) A signed statement of claim. This form requires the beneficiary to certify that he or she is the person listed on the policy as the beneficiary, and sets out which policy, identified by its number, is being claimed.

3) A death certificate to establish the death and identity of the deceased.

4) The policy. It has no intrinsic value but the companies like to get settled policies out of circulation.

If the policy is less than five years old, the company may ask for an attending physician's statement confirming that a significant medical problem was not withheld when the insurance was arranged If the policy is less than two years old, the possibility of suicide – which invalidates the policy within this period – will be considered. In this case, a coroner's report could be required. If death occurs outside Canada, the insurer could require the body to be returned to Canada for identification. Most claims are uncomplicated and can usually be settled within a month. The settlement cheque should include interest from the death date to the settlement date.

Claiming a disability benefit

Disability claims are more complicated and stressful than death claims. For one thing, you are sick or injured, so insurance paperwork will not be welcome. For another, you will have to deal with the fine print of the policy – or a multitude of policies. And if you are covered by more than one policy, qualifications may well differ.

Each policy defines "disability" and to qualify for benefits you must satisfy that definition. One policy might pay until you are back on the job and working with full effectiveness. Another might pay briefly, then cut you off as soon as you return to the office, even if it's for the lightest of duties.

"Own occupation" policies are the simplest to qualify for, since it's usually clear if you can do, or are doing, your regular job. With this insurance you need only prove that you can't do your regular job, and provide medical evidence that it is an accident or sickness that prevents you from performing. You will have to report your medical condition every month. If you are claiming a residual benefit you will have to provide a comprehensive report on your income pattern for the several years before disability and a monthly report on your earned income, if any, during disability. And by the way, not everyone suffers a loss of income when disabled. The owner of a large business might very well continue at full salary even though he does not set foot in the office. With some policies he will collect benefits, with others he will not.

Unless it is clear that your disability is long term, you and your doctor will have to complete monthly reports. If there are questions about the claim, you may have to visit a company-appointed physician for a review of your health history and recovery process.

Canada's disability insurance companies can generally be relied on to honour their contracts. By contrast, many companies in the United States issue policies with so many clauses and restrictions that it's doubtful whether they intend to pay many claims. However, don't expect your company to ignore the wording of its policies. If the policy requires that you not be gainfully employed as long as you are receiving benefits, don't expect it to pay if you are. Disability insurers have been hard-hit by the recent recession. My experience shows that obtaining benefits may require some pressure from you or your agent. You may even need legal advice.

CHAPTER 22

Seven Personal Profiles

THIS IS NOT A DO-IT-YOURSELF book. By now, you have some firm ideas on how much of what type of insurance you need. But you need an agent to refine your ideas, to implement them and to provide continuing service.

The life insurance industry can be competitive, especially if you insist on it. You can and should tell your agent, up front, that you want an insurance proposal tailored to your needs and personality, at a competitive price. Chapter eleven contains sufficient rate information, especially in the buyer's guides to insurance, for you to detect needlessly expensive insurance.

For family insurance, the beneficiary should play an active role in the discussions and considerations. The insurance, after all, is for the protection and benefit of the beneficiary. If you are the beneficiary of a life insurance policy, either corporately or within the family, you should ask to be made an "irrevocable beneficiary." This means the policy owner can't cancel the policy, pledge it to the bank or change the beneficiary to a secret partner, without your written consent. If such an attempt is made, you will be notified.

We hope we have made the point strongly enough that there is no such thing as one type of life insurance for all people in all situations. Anyone who tells you so is deceiving you. Term insurance, term-to-100, whole life and universal life are all the correct answers to particular insurance needs – and dead wrong in others.

As a knowledgeable consumer, you have at your disposal an impressive array of agents, companies, services and products. The life insurance industry has people who are eager for your business and willing to provide superlative service to earn it. All you have to do is hire and direct. The knowledge you have picked up in *Insure Sensibly* will help you command the expertise and service you deserve.

Seven personal profiles

The following scenarios are genuine situations. The considerations and results are also genuine. However, premiums and policies change over time. Therefore, the products the clients actually chose are similar to those illustrated but they may not be identical.

David and Ann Nakamura

David and Ann Nakamura, age twenty-four and twenty-five, work in the computer department of a major electronics manufacturer. Newly married, they wanted to arrange insurance because Ann was expecting their first child. David's father, also a client, had taught his son that responsible parenthood included provision of an income for his wife and child should he die prematurely.

David and Ann were debt-free and had accumulated $25,000 in mutual funds which they planned to use to buy a house. They decided that $400,000 of protection on David and $250,000 on Ann would be appropriate, and a survey of renewable term and term-to-100 indicated that renewable term was the better choice. They wanted to keep the initial cost as low as possible as they continued to save for a house.

The Nakamuras each had group life insurance of a year's salary. More group coverage was available, but the cost was higher than the premiums on the individual policies they could buy. Of course, their own insurance also has the advantage of remaining with them if they change jobs.

The ten-year term policies appeared to offer better value than five-year. They chose American Life after considering initial cost, future renewals and guarantees. Reliable Life offered lower initial premiums, but the attractive renewal rates quoted require the passing of future medicals, and the Nakamuras were advised that the risk was not worth the savings. Primerica's rates were attractive but the conversion right expires at age twenty-nine. Transamerica's early rates were excellent but much higher than American's in the renewal period.

For Ann, we had to go to the seventh-best company in terms of initial premium. This is because American Life, like many other insurance companies, offered an additional saving on policies bought for a husband and wife. By insuring both on the same policy, they saved an administration cost of about $75 a year. Ann and David chose to have their monthly premiums automatically deducted from

Survey of Policies for David Nakamura

10-year renewable term
Male
Face amount: $400,000
Age last birthday: 24   Age nearest birthday: 24   Preferred non-smoker

Reliable Life Insurance Company
YRT-95 (Star)-level premiums 1-10

	Current	Guaranteed
Age 24		$ 356
Age 34	$672	1,604
Age 35	712	1,608
Age 36	756	1,616
Age 37	808	1,628
Age 38	864	1,648

Renewable to 95   Convertible to 34

Reliable Life Insurance Company
YRT-95 (Gold)-level premiums 1-10

	Current	Guaranteed
Age 24		$ 356
Age 34	$728*	1,604
Age 35	764*	1,608
Age 36	796*	1,616
Age 37	832*	1,628
Age 38	880*	1,648

Renewable to 95   Convertible to 65

Primerica Life Insurance Company
ZPL-Eagle 10G-10-year R & C term

	Guaranteed
Age 24	$ 358
Age 34	714
Age 44	1,062
Age 54	2,514
Age 64	5,970
Age 70	10,958

Becomes ART to age 90 at age 70
Renewable to 90 Convertible to 29

American International Assurance Life
Term Plus - 10-year R & C term

	Guaranteed
Age 24	$ 424
Age 34	532
Age 44	1,064
Age 54	2,560
Age 64	6,332
Age 74	12,412

Original age enhancement (rate) option
Renewable to 75   Convertible to 65

London Life Insurance Company
10-year term non-participating R&C

	Guaranteed
Age 24	$ 431.00
Age 34	489.00
Age 44	1,019.00
Age 54	2,333.50
Age 64	6,309.75
Age 74	15,462.50

Renewable to70 Convertible to 65

Sun Life Assurance Company
10-year renewable term

	Guaranteed
Age 24	$ 435
Age 44	1,111
Age 54	2,615
Age 64	6,819
Age 74	13,435

Renewable to 75 Convertible to 65

Legend: * value projected, not guaranteed

SOURCE: COMPULIFE SOFTWARE INC.   AUGUST 1995

TABLE XXI

Survey of Policies for Ann Nakamura

10-year renewable term
Female
Face amount: $250,000
Age last birthday: 25   Age nearest birthday: 25   Preferred non-smoker

Westbury Canadian Life Insurance		Financial Life Assurance Company	
Term 10 - 10-year R&C term		Choice Term 10	
	Guaranteed		Guaranteed
Age 25	$ 192.50	Age 25	$ 215
Age 35	347.50	Age 35	390
Age 45	597.50	Age 40	580
Age 55	1,432.50	Age 45	820
Age 65	3,345.00	Age 50	1,085
Age 75	11,207.50	Age 55	1,490

GIC option included for ages up to 55

Renewable to 80   Convertible to 70   Renewable to 80   Convertible to 65

Metropolitan Life Insurance		Empire Life Insurance Company	
Executive Term 10 - 10-year R & C		Term 10/10	
	Guaranteed		Guaranteed
Age 25	$ 217.50	Age 25	$ 217.50
Age 35	267.50	Age 35	317.50
Age 45	610.00		
Age 55	1,435.00		
Age 65	4,460.00		
Age 75	9,630.00		

Renewable to 80 Convertible to 65   Renewable to 45 Convertible to 35

Transamerica Life Insurance Co.		Laurier Life Insurance Company	
10-year convertible & renewable		UltraTerm 10 - 10-year R & C Term	
	Guaranteed		Guaranteed
Age 25	$ 217.50	Age 25	$ 219.50
Age 35	420.00	Age 35	287.00
Age 45	752.50	Age 45	502.00
Age 55	1,697.50	Age 55	1,467.00
Age 65	4,000.00	Age 65	3,699.50
Age 75	8,965.00		

Renewable to 80 Convertible to 71   Renewable to 75 Convertible to 65

SOURCE: COMPULIFE SOFTWARE INC.   AUGUST 1995

TABLE XXII

their bank account, a service offered by all companies. The monthly premium is about 9 percent of the annual premium.

Although American offers another product which is less expensive, this policy is only convertible and renewable to age forty-five without further medical examinations.

Jennifer and Ian Baines

Jennifer and Ian are young newlyweds in their late teens. Both smoke. This young couple already had a child and Jennifer is expecting their second. Ian works as a general labourer for a metal fabricating company. Jennifer tends to their child and mobile home. Money is scarce and a survey of five- and ten-year policies found that $100,000 of protection would cost about $200 or more a year, or $18 a month, increasing at five-year intervals.

However, Toronto Mutual offers a policy that has a level premium to age thirty, then renews every five years. Such a policy doesn't fit any of the typical categories that can be compared in a computer survey. (Many companies have such policies designed to fit the particular needs of a small number of people.) Toronto Mutual's policy guarantees both the face amount and the premiums to age seventy with a level premium of only $206 until Ian reaches age thirty-two.

Ian and Jennifer are debt-free but the $100,000 of insurance is still inadequate. It would provide Jennifer with an investment income of less than half the income Ian can earn but their budget precludes a more satisfactory level of protection.

Steve and Carol Krol

Steve and Carol Krol, age thirty and twenty-nine, are civil servants. He's a property assessor; she's a school nurse. After six years of owning a house they still have a $55,000 mortgage but the value of the property has quadrupled. They have few financial concerns and no debt other than the mortgage. They have two children.

Steve and Carol had group life insurance at work and another $100,000 of group coverage from the University of Toronto Alumni Association, but they knew they needed more. Steve had sold life insurance for almost two years, and had strong opinions on what he wanted and what he didn't. He was dead against term insurance, since the cost would increase at each renewal to levels that eventually would be prohibitively expensive. He wanted a policy with cash values he could use in retirement.

5-Year Renewable Term Survey for Steve Krol

Male
Face amount: $400,000
Age last birthday: 30   Age nearest birthday: 30   Preferred non-smoker

---

Sun Life Assurance Company
5-year renewable & convertible

	Guaranteed
Age 30	$ 355
Age 35	419
Age 40	627
Age 45	1,075
Age 50	1,647
Age 55	2,519

Renewable to 75 Convertible to 65

Laurier Life Insurance Company
UltraTerm 5 – 5-year R & C

	Guaranteed
Age 30	$ 417.50
Age 35	509.50
Age 40	737.50
Age 45	1,077.50
Age 50	1,629.50
Age 55	2,533.50

Renewable to 75 Convertible to 65

Mutual Life Assurance of Canada
5-year renewable term pro

	Reduced	Maximum
Age 30		$ 424
Age 35	$ 504*	985
Age 40	712*	1,345
Age 45	1,084*	2,013
Age 50	1,604*	3,081
Age 55	2,476*	4,977

Reduced premium – max. less dividend
Renewable to 75 Convertible to 65

Investors Syndicate
Term 5 – 5-year R & C

	Regular
Age 30	$ 429
Age 35	485
Age 40	645
Age 45	993
Age 50	1.545
Age 55	2,369

Renewable to 70 Convertible to 65

Great-West Life Assurance Co.
Term 5 – 5-year R & C

	Regular
Age 30	$ 429
Age 35	485
Age 40	645
Age 45	993
Age 50	1,545
Age 55	2,369

Renewable to 70 Convertible to 65

Transamerica Life Insurance Co.
5-year convertible & renewable

	Guaranteed
Age 30	$ 430
Age 35	662
Age 40	778
Age 45	1,094
Age 50	1,558
Age 55	2,230

Renewable to 80 Convertible to 71

Legend: * value projected, not guaranteed

TABLE XXIII

A laptop computer was set up on the Krol's kitchen table and used to survey various types of insurance. This allowed them to compare the savings of competitive term-to-100 policies with whole life policies. Steve was shocked at the disparity in price for similar policies.

From his experience as an agent, he knew that many, if not most, older people prefer to keep their life insurance in force even though they had bought cash-value insurance with retirement in mind. The Krols had not been funding their RRSPs to the maximum; and were advised that it would make sense to do so. In addition to the RRSP contributions, they could make other unsheltered investments so that at retirement they would be able to keep their insurance in force.

A comparison showed that a competitive five-year term policy cost $96,192 more than term-to-100 by age seventy-five on an interest-adjusted basis, that is, assuming the initial savings were invested at 7 percent interest. Not only did the renewable term cost more, but it held out the unpleasant prospect of $6,723- and $11,071-a-year premiums at the older ages – and might run out before death. Table XXV shows the details of this comparison.

Westbury Canadian offered a low-cost, guaranteed premium term-to-100 policy that was compared to the other choices available. This policy, at $1,120 a year for life, guaranteed $400,000 at death, but had no cash or paid-up value.

Term-to-100 (Guaranteed) Survey for Steve Krol

Male
Face amount: $400,000
Age last birthday: 30   Age nearest birthday: 30   Preferred non-smoker

Westbury Canadian Life	**Royal Life Insurance Company**
T-100 plus T10 alternative	Term-100
Premium: $1,120	Premium: $1,164
(includes CSV option at end of 10th year, equal to difference between T10 and Term 100 Plus, without interest)	
Aeterna Life Insurance Company	**Transamerica Life Insurance Co.**
T-100 Pure	Term to 100 – without paid-up values
Premium: $1,170	Premium: $1,170
(provides a 90-day grace period following 5th policy year. Waiver premium: 4 month waiting period)	(Option available which provides cash and reduced paid-up values after 20th policy year)

SOURCE: COMPULIFE SOFTWARE INC.   OCTOBER 1995

TABLE XXIV

Interest-Adjusted Cost Analysis for Steve Krol

Face amount: $400,000
Interest assumption: 7%

Year	Age	Sun Life 5-yr. R&C	Westbury Canadian T100 Plus	Difference in premiums	Premiums saved with interest
1	30	$ 355	$1,120	($ 765)	($ 794.45)
3	32	355	1,120	(765)	(2,476.29)
5	34	355	1,120	(765)	(4,290.13)
7	36	419	1,120	(701)	(6,110.83)
9	38	419	1,120	(701)	(8,074.09)
11	40	627	1,120	(493)	(9,976.13)
13	42	627	1,120	(493)	(11,802.75)
15	44	627	1,120	(493)	(13,772.73)
17	46	1,075	1,120	(45)	(14,948.91)
19	48	1,075	1,120	(45)	(16,217.39)
21	50	1,647	1,120	527	(16,991.41)
23	52	1,647	1,120	527	(17,209.29)
25	54	1,647	1,120	527	(17,444.26)
27	56	2,519	1,120	1,399	(15,851.67)
29	58	2,519	1,120	1,399	(14,134.09)
31	60	3,967	1,120	2,847	(10,777.95)
33	62	3,967	1,120	2,847	(5,596.78)
35	64	3,967	1,120	2,847	(8.98)
37	66	6,723	1,120	5,603	11,851.76
39	68	6,723	1,120	5,603	24,643.37
41	70	11,071	1,120	9,951	42,954.28
43	72	11,071	1,120	9,951	67,391.52
45	74	11,071	1,120	9,951	93,746.65
46	75	0	1,120	(1,120)	96,192.78

SOURCE: COMPULIFE SOFTWARE INC.   OCTOBER 1995

TABLE XXV

When Steve studied the surveys of guaranteed whole life, he noted that one of the cheapest policies (offered by Empire Life), at $1,270 a year, guaranteed a $64,000 cash value at age sixty-five if it was cancelled. He knew he was not likely to cancel the policy but he couldn't help asking the question: Is $150 a year worth the option of a $64,000 cash value? (At 7 percent the savings would compound to $22,187.) He concluded it was. The Krols applied for Empire Life's Solution 100 guaranteed whole life insurance.

Term-to-100 (Guaranteed) Survey for R. Surminski

Face amount: $750,000
Male
Age last birthday: 47   Age nearest birthday: 47   Preferred non-smoker

Equitable Life Insurance Company
Select Term-to-100
Premium: $6,067.50
Automatic increase benefit increases
face amt & premium 5% per year for
years 2 – 5. Can be cancelled by insured
at any time.

Laurier Life Insurance Company
Permachoice Bronze - life pay
Premium: $6,264.50
Provides a living benefit option.
Available as pay-to-65, -70, -85,
20-pay or graduated pay.

Transamerica Life Insurance Co.
Term-to-100 - w/o paid-up values
Premium: $6,282.50
Another option is available which
provides cash and reduced paid-up
values after 20th policy year

Seaboard Life Insurance Company
T-100-Retro - guaranteed term-to-100
Premium: $6,365
Convertible to U.L. at any age but Retro has
a special 5th, 6th or 7th year conversion to
universal life.

TABLE XXVI

Richard Surminski

Richard Surminski, age forty-seven, phoned to complain that his term insurance was about to renew at a premium almost double the previous rate. He was anxious not to face even more expensive premiums in the future. Surminski had an old term policy – so old that it predated the change to smokers' and non-smokers' rates. If he had been a smoker, his insurance would have been well priced, but as a non-smoker he could do much better. He was in good health, and said he would have no trouble qualifying for new insurance. (If he had been in poor health, he could have considered conversion to a permanent policy. The rules of his current insurance company, however, would have required him to pay smokers' rates for the new policy since the old policy was not at non-smokers' rates. This would have been expensive.)

A survey of ten-year term revealed that the lowest premiums were from Colonia, Empire and Transamerica. Colonia has a poor solvency rating with TRAC, passing only three of eight tests. Empire Life renews only once and is convertible only to age 57. Mr. Surminski concluded that his best choice for ten-year term would be the policy from Transamerica. Its TRAC rating is eight out of eight

10-Year Renewable Term Survey for R. Surminski

Face amount: $750,000
Male
Age last birthday: 47   Age nearest birthday: 47   Preferred non-smoker

Colonia Life Insurance Company 10-year R & C Term	Guaranteed	Empire Life Insurance Company Term 10/10	Guaranteed
Age 47	$1,897.50	Age 47	$1,947.50
Age 57	7,477.50	Age 57	7,415.00
Age 67	16,920.00		

Renewable to 75 Convertible to 65   Renewable to 67 Convertible to 57

Transamerica Life Insurance Co. 10-year convertible and renewable	Guaranteed	Colonia Life Insurance Company Escalating 10-year R & C term	Guaranteed
Age 47	$ 1,947.50	Age 47	$ 1,952.50
Age 57	7,797.50	Age 57	7,600.00
Age 67	20,277,50	Age 67	17,387.50
Age 77	45,852.50		

Renewable to 80 Convertible to 71   Renewable to 75 Convertible to 65

Equitable Life Insurance Company 10-year renewable and convertible	Guaranteed	Gerling Global Life Insurance Co. Term 10 – 10-year renewable term	Guaranteed
Age 47	$ 1,955.00	Age 47	$ 1,960.00
Age 57	6,050.00	Age 57	7,900.00
Age 67	16,662.50	Age 67	17,950.00

SOURCE: COMPULIFE SOFTWARE INC.   OCTOBER 1995

TABLE XXVII

and its A.M. Best rating is A+ (Colonia's is A– and Empire's is A). Transamerica's term policy is renewable to 80 and convertible to 71.

When he saw the term-to-100 quotes, he became excited. The guaranteed level premium for the rest of his life cost only a few hundred dollars more than his current five-year term rate. And, in five years the term-to-100 premium would be a bargain in comparison. Most of Richard's retirement income will come from a University of Toronto pension. Continued cheap term-to-100 would allow him more flexibility in choosing income options. Although he was married, he could elect an income on his life alone, secure in the knowledge that an additional $750,000 of tax-free cash is guaranteed for his wife.

Surminski chose to lock in both the $750,000 benefit and the guaranteed level premium by choosing Transamerica's term-to-100 policy. In earlier years, any of the four companies with the lowest premiums would have been a good choice. With the recent collapse of Sovereign, Les Cooperants and Confederation, and the sudden merger of North American Life, solvency is a major concern in making a recommendation. A permanent policy is only as permanent as the company. In this case, according to both TRAC and A.M. Best, Transamerica had a better rating than the other companies on the first page of the Compulife survey.

David MacTaggart

MacTaggart, age fifty-one, and a group of colleagues had made a joint investment and needed life insurance to cover their business loan; MacTaggart's share was $450,000. The loan was expected to be outstanding for a number of years; and he wanted to make sure his insurance choice was economical in the long run. However, another member of the business group wanted to buy "cheap" insurance.

A computer comparison of yearly renewable, five-year renewable, ten-year renewable, twenty-year renewable and term-to-100 insurance was prepared. The initial and renewal premiums from the best choice of each type can be seen in Table XXVIII. The total cost of the policies over the next twenty years was then converted to a single lump sum and discounted at 7 percent to a present value. That is, each stream of payments was converted to the equivalent value of a single payment in current dollars. The present value table of twenty years of premiums is also included in this table.

This table makes it clear why we tend to recommend the ten-year term as a compromise of affordable initial premium and long-term value. The yearly renewable term policy has a very low initial premium, but the renewals are such that the plan is practical only for five years, or less.

A Survey of Policies for a Business Group

ANNUAL PREMIUMS

Type	Years 1 - 5	Years 6 - 10	Years 11 - 15	Years 16 - 20
Yearly term	$837	$2,867	$11,930	$17,343
Five-year term	1,513	2,440	6,611	10,153
Ten-year term	1,657	1,657	7,349	7,349
Twenty-year term	2,605	2,605	2,605	2,605
Term-to-100	4,717	4,717	4,717	4,717

THE PRESENT VALUE OF TWENTY YEARS OF PREMIUMS

Type	Present value
Yearly term	$65,471.15
Five-year term	45,159.99
Ten-year term	40,530.50
Twenty-year term	29,529.23
Term-to-100	53,475.67

TABLE XXVIII

Since there were thirty-two members in MacTaggart's business group, each requiring insurance ranging from $250,000 to $800,000, a discount was arranged with an insurance company, Financial Life. The group agreed to pay the cost of ten-year term for each member; those who wanted their insurance to remain in force after the group business was wound up were allowed to buy term-to-100, paying the initial premium difference personally. About half the members elected for the term-to-100 option.

Dr. Gerard LaPierre

Gerard LaPierre, age sixty-nine, has worked all of his career in a small logging town in northern Ontario. He had helped a local real estate developer open a subdivision and, when the developer had died, the doctor found himself carrying on with the project on his own. He was enjoying the venture, and making more money than ever before.

When the recession hit in 1990, however, Dr. LaPierre was stuck with a large inventory of land. He owned it outright, so there was no pressure to sell, but he had assumed the project would be complete before he turned seventy. It was now clear that it would be several

Whole Life (Guaranteed) Survey for Dr. LaPierre

Face amount: $700,000
Male   Age last birthday: 69   Age nearest birthday: 69
Preferred non-smoker   Premiums payable to 100

Financial Life Insurance Company		**The Empire Life Insurance Co.**	
PERMATERM +(Non-smoker rate)		Solution 100 - with ROP and RPU	
Premium: $25,792		Premium: $26,825	
Cash values	Guaranteed	Cash values	Guaranteed
10 years	$ 86,800		
15 years	191,100	15 years	$ 70,700
20 years	289,800	20 years	246,400
Paid-up values	Guaranteed	Paid-up values	Guaranteed
20 years	443,100	20 years	281,400
		Policy offers return of premium	
For higher values or shorter premium		(cash values) and reduced paid values	
paying period, refer to Choice Life		in 15 years (earlier at older ages)	
Standard Life Assurance Company		**Transamerica Life Insurance Co.**	
SLT - Standard Life Term-100		Term-to-100 w/cash + paid-up values	
Premium: $26,868		Premium: $27,021	
Cash values	Guaranteed	Cash values	Guaranteed
20 years	$331,100	20 years	$320,600
Paid-up values	Guaranteed	Paid-up values	Guaranteed
20 years	413,000	20 years	425,600
		Cash values and reduced paid-up	
		values are available after the 20th	
		policy year	

SOURCE: COMPULIFE   OCTOBER 1995

TABLE XXIX

years before the land was all developed, and, therefore, several years before it could be sold.

He was concerned about the capital gains tax that would be triggered by his death. His wife was in no position to carry on the business, and he would want her to sell the property. If she had to accept financing, she could be caught owing a lot of tax for which she had little cash. Dr. LaPierre had a renewable term policy that he had renewed every five years, each time convinced that it would be

---

Term-to-100 (Guaranteed) Survey for Dr. LaPierre

Manufacturers Life Insurance Co.
Signet

Premium: $23,398.00

Maritime Life Assurance Company
Term to 100

Premium: $25,810.00

Laurier Life Insurance Company
Permachoice Bronze - life pay

Premium: $26,475.50

Policy provides a living benefit
option. Policy is available in a
number of payment options:
Pay-to-65, -70, -85, 20-pay or
graduated pay.

Transamerica Life Insurance Co.
Term to 100 - without paid-up values

Premium: $26,545.00

Another option is available which
provides cash and reduced
paid-up values after the 20th
policy year.

SOURCE: COMPULIFE SOFTWARE INC.   OCTOBER 1995

TABLE XXX

the last renewal. But, every time he found it important to keep the insurance as collateral on loans or to cover potential capital gains tax. The policy was no longer convertible to permanent insurance.

A survey of permanent life insurance showed that there was not much difference between term-to-100 and whole life at Dr. LaPierre's age, so the best choice would be the one that provided the most options — whole life insurance. The cheapest whole life policy was available from Financial Life. He looked forward to gradually selling his real estate holdings and paying the taxes out of the profits realized. Since he was quite wealthy, and would have plenty of cash after the property was sold, he envisioned not needing the life insurance in a few years. The whole life insurance cost only about five percent more than term-to-100, so he opted for the guaranteed whole life from Standard Life. Standard offered the best compromise of solvency rating, premium and cash value. That way, he would be able to receive a refund of some of his premiums when he cancelled the insurance.

Giovanni and Maria DiMarco

Giovanni and Maria DiMarco, aged sixty-three and fifty-eight, had invested in small apartment buildings over their working careers,

Joint-Life/Last-to-Die Proposal

Presented to Mr. & Mrs. DiMarco
NN Financial's Protector Plus
Face amount: $1,000,000
First life: Male non-smoker   Age last birthday: 63
Second life: Female non-smoker   Age last birthday: 58

Plan	Annual premium	Monthly premium
Protector Plus	$ 8,320	$44.645

Year	Guaranteed cash values	Guaranteed paid-up values
20	$42,000	$77,000
25	50,000	82,000
30	61,000	88,000

Note: cash and paid-up values begin in 20th policy year

TABLE XXXI

eventually finding themselves with a substantial estate. Most of the buildings were in Toronto and likely to continue to be excellent investments. The DiMarcos wanted to leave the buildings to their children and were concerned about the capital gains tax payable at their death.

Mr. DiMarco had been advised that he needed to arrange $1,000,000 of permanent insurance. The couple were certain that they would never want to cancel this insurance, so term-to-100 was the only permanent protection they wanted to buy. Because capital gains tax is not payable until the death of the second spouse, term-to-100 was much cheaper if bought on the life of Mrs. DiMarco, who was five years younger than her husband.

But, many companies issue joint policies payable when the second person dies and these are even cheaper than a policy on the younger spouse. NN Financial quoted $8,320 a year on a joint policy compared with Empire Life's $13,520 for a policy on her life – a significant savings, especially when she is likely to be the second to die.

CHAPTER 23

Obtaining More Information

THE CANADIAN LIFE AND Health Insurance Association, a national body of life insurance companies, offers free booklets and pamphlets not only on life and disability insurance but on estate planning, retirement planning and other aspects of personal finance. The address is:

Communications Department
Canadian Life and Health Insurance Association
1 Queen St. E., Suite 1700
Toronto, Ontario M5C 2X9
You can call the association's consumer information service free from anywhere in Canada by dialling 1-800-268-8099. The service operates from 9 a.m. to 5 p.m. (Toronto time) on business days.

The Life Underwriters Association of Canada is a national group of insurance agents, each of whom represents one company, in most cases. The Independent Life Insurance Brokers of Canada is a younger and smaller group representing the interests of brokers who sell the products of several insurance companies.

Life Underwriters Association of Canada
41 Lesmill Road
Don Mills, Ontario M3B 2T3
Phone: (416) 444-5251
Fax: (416) 444-8031

Independent Life Insurance Brokers of Canada
2175 Sheppard Ave. East, Suite 310
Willowdale, Ontario M2J 1W8
Phone: (416) 491-9747
Fax: (416) 491-1670

Regulatory authorities

Life insurance companies in Canada are regulated by both the federal and provincial governments. Each jurisdiction can incorporate companies, and each regulates the solvency of the companies it has incorporated. Provincial governments regulate all matters of contract – premium rates, advertising, the wording of contracts and similar matters. The solvency of companies operating in Canada on a branch basis is exclusively regulated by Ottawa. Both jurisdictions have facilities for taking complaints from the public. But since the provinces have jurisdiction over contracts, disputes over the wording of insurance policies should be directed to provincial authorities. Here are the life insurance regulators:

Federal Government
Superintendent of Financial Institutions
255 Albert St., 16th floor
Ottawa, Ontario K1A 0H2
Phone: (613) 990-8010
Fax: (613) 952-8219

Alberta
Superintendent of Insurance
Alberta Treasury
Room 200, 9515 - 107 Street
Edmonton, Alberta T5K 2C3
Phone: (403) 422-1592
Fax: (403) 427-3033

British Columbia
Superintendent of Insurance
Ministry of Finance and Corporate Relations
1050 West Pender St., Suite 1900
Vancouver, British Columbia V6E 3S7
Phone: (604) 660-2947
Fax: (604) 660-3170

Manitoba
Superintendent of Insurance
405 Broadway Ave., Room 1142
Winnipeg, Manitoba R3C 3L6
Phone: (204) 945-2542
Fax: (204) 948-2268

New Brunswick
Superintendent of Insurance
Centennial Building, Room 477
P.O. Box 6000
Fredericton, New Brunswick E3B 5H1
Phone: (506) 453-2512
Fax: (506) 453-2613

Newfoundland
Superintendent of Insurance
2nd floor, 100 Elizabeth Avenue
P.O. Box 8700
St. John's, Newfoundland A1B 4J6
Phone: (709) 729-2594
Fax: (709) 729-6998

Northwest Territories
Superintendent of Insurance
Ministry of Justice
Box 1320
Yellowknife, Northwest Territories X1A 2L9
Phone: (403) 920-8054
Fax: (403) 873-0272

Nova Scotia
Superintendent of Insurance
Department of Finance
P.O. Box 187
Halifax, Nova Scotia B2J 2N3
Phone: (902) 424-6331
Fax: (902) 424-8652

Ontario
Superintendent of Insurance
Ontario Insurance Commission
17th floor, 5160 Yonge Street
Box 85
North York, Ontario M2N 6L9
Phone: (416) 250-6750
Fax: (416) 590-7073

Prince Edward Island
Superintendent of Insurance
Ministry of Justice
Shaw Building, 73 Rochford St.
P.O. Box 2000
Charlottetown, Prince Edward Island C1A 7N8
Phone: (902) 368-4564
Fax: (902) 368-5283

Quebec
Superintendent of Insurance
Suite 801, 800 Place d'Youville
Quebec City, Quebec G1R 4Y5
Phone: (418) 694-5011
Fax: (418) 528-0835

Saskatchewan
Superintendent of Insurance
Consumer Protection Branch
1871 Smith Street
Regina, Saskatchewan S4P 3V7
Phone: (306) 787-7881
Fax: (306) 787-8999

Yukon Territory
Superintendent of Insurance
Ministry of Consumer and Corporate Affairs
3rd floor, 2134 Second Avenue
P.O. Box 2703
Whitehorse, Yukon Y1A 2C6
Phone: (403) 667-5257

Index

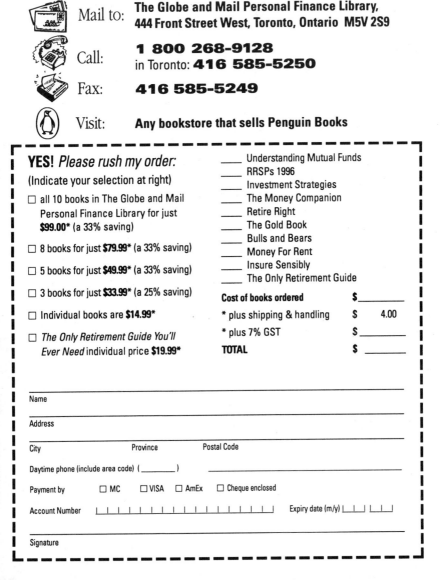